# The Soul Journeyer's Companion

## A Cosmic Re-memoir

### Book II of the Journey OM Series

Shima

All efforts have been made to acknowledge and contact the copyright holders of material used in the writing of *The Soul Journeyer's Companion*. If we have unknowingly infringed copyright in any way, we offer our sincere apologies and will make appropriate acknowledgement in future editions.

Text Design: J. K. Eckert & Company, Inc.

Photography: Jim Kelly

Editor: Teresa Brady

Cover Design: Mike Clark

Artist: James G. Kelly IV

Peace Waters Publishing
First Edition

ISBN: 978-0-9835675-0-9

Printed in the United States of America

*To my Mom, Beverly,*

*Who walks the way of Chief White Bird,*

*Cherishing independence above all,*

*Refusing to surrender for fear of freedom's forfeit.*

*You have taught me the true Wisdom of*

*Chief Joseph's words,*

*"All paths are the right path and all lead to One."*

### *AS ALL JOURNEYS DO*

*It started out as all journeys do*
*One—*
*Searching for two.*

*With book in hand and compass in another,*
*Leaving one shore for another.*

*The journey begins as all journeys do*
*One—*
*Searching for two.*

*Days turn into nights;*
*Nights into weeks.*
*After months no destination found.*

*The destination begins as all journeys do*
*One—*
*Searching for two.*

*Advice is given*
*In many languages all along the way.*
*Explaining every day*
*That all journeys,*
*Sometimes—*
*End as they began*
*One—*
*Searching for two.*

*With the Lord's book in one hand*
*And God's compass in the other,*
*One now equals—*
*Two—*
*God and You.*

—Jim Kelly

This book may change your life, your energy and your atomic structure. You will come face-to-face with your "I AM" Presence. If you are willing to release every belief system you have ever valued and move into the Light of Grace that is your true Self, it will be a perfect read. *The Soul Journeyer's Companion* is an invitation to remember and realize your human-divine identity through the experience of one soul journeyer.

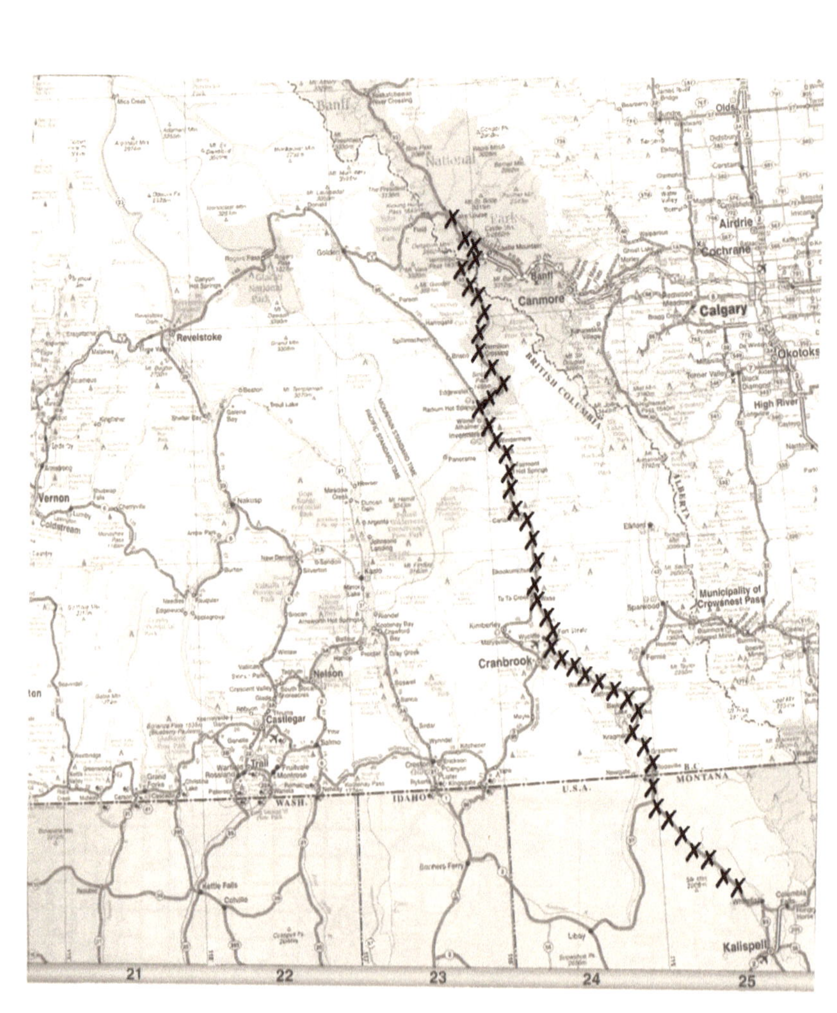

Banff
National
Park
Airdrie
Cochrane
Calgary
Okotoks
High River
BRITISH COLUMBIA
ALBERTA
Revelstoke
Golden
Banff
Canmore
Vernon
Coldstream
Nakusp
Panorama
Radium Hot Springs
Invermere
Municipality of
Crowsnest Pass
Nelson
Kaslo
Kimberley
Cranbrook
Fernie
Castlegar
Trail
Montrose
WASH.
IDAHO
U.S.A.
MONTANA
B.C.
Kettle Falls
Bonners Ferry
Libby
Kalispell
21
22
23
24
25

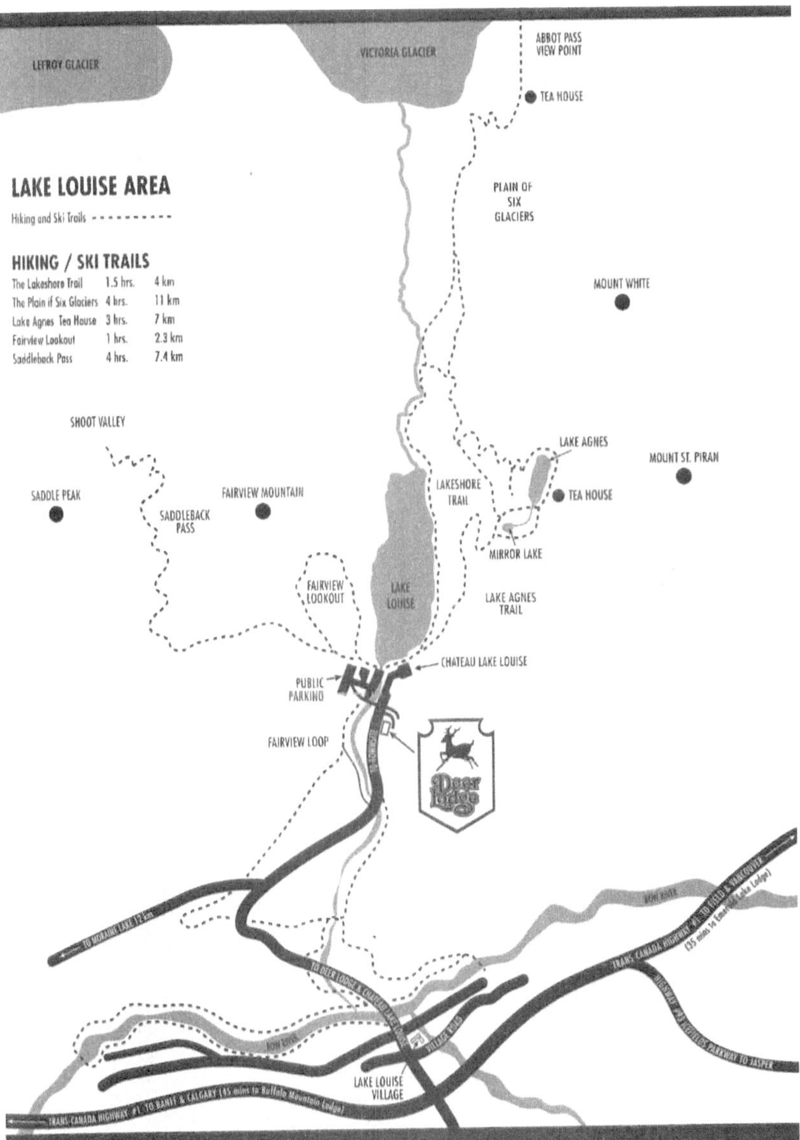

LEFROY GLACIER
VICTORIA GLACIER
ABBOT PASS VIEW POINT
TEA HOUSE
PLAIN OF SIX GLACIERS
LAKE LOUISE AREA
Hiking and Ski Trails
HIKING / SKI TRAILS
The Lakeshore Trail      1.5 hrs.      4 km
The Plain if Six Glaciers      4 hrs.      11 km
Lake Agnes Tea House      3 hrs.      7 km
Fairview Lookout      1 hrs.      2.3 km
Saddleback Pass      4 hrs.      7.4 km
MOUNT WHITE
SHOOT VALLEY
LAKE AGNES
MOUNT ST. PIRAN
SADDLE PEAK
FAIRVIEW MOUNTAIN
LAKESHORE TRAIL
TEA HOUSE
SADDLEBACK PASS
MIRROR LAKE
FAIRVIEW LOOKOUT
LAKE LOUISE
LAKE AGNES TRAIL
CHATEAU LAKE LOUISE
PUBLIC PARKING
FAIRVIEW LOOP
Deer Lodge
BOW RIVER
TRANS-CANADA HIGHWAY #1 TO FIELD & VANCOUVER (35 mins to Emerald Lake Lodge)
TO MORAINE LAKE 12 km
TO DEER LODGE & CHATEAU LAKE LOUISE
ICEFIELDS PARKWAY TO JASPER
BOW RIVER
VILLAGE ROAD
LAKE LOUISE VILLAGE
TRANS-CANADA HIGHWAY #1 TO BANFF & CALGARY (45 mins to Buffalo Mountain Lodge)

# CONTENTS

## MONDAY, AUGUST 10



## SOMETIME IN THE FUTURE

# *PRELUDE*

I begin this journey like the last…well, no…not really. In *Journey OM, A Soul Journeyer's Adventure* you met me on the threshold of the fifth dimension with a lot to learn. A lot! I was, as the saying goes, on the proverbial fence, straddling dimensions with a foot in each. Upon my return from the Chief Joseph stargate pilgrimage there was no stepping back into the third dimension, and there were no trail markers going forward. The earth-worn path had become a Light stream that only my higher consciousness could travel. Once I'd said Yes to God there was no stopping my spiritual evolution. In this cosmic re-memoir, I share the homecoming of my soul. It is my telling of my passage to enlightenment; my experience of becoming a Divine-Human being and remembering who *I AM* and who we all are—in Oneness. My story—my experience—is a helpful teaching tool if you find yourself seeking a similar Light stream.

This book is not of the third dimension, or the fourth, or even the fifth dimension. Its musings and remembrances ebb and flow through all dimensions. It is omni-dimensional. *The Soul Journeyer's Companion, A Cosmic Re-memoir* is birthed from the music of the spheres where language limits Light's Wisdom. Words take me only so far in describing my evolution; it is when the words fall short that Light shines forth. Such is the magic herein. You too will receive the Light encodings if you are open and willing to the possibility that you are Spirit dwelling in a physical body.

Depending upon the level of your consciousness, you may find this read startling, inconceivable or even incomprehensible. Then you should put it down. It will not serve you. But if, as you read, you feel an inkling of familiarity, a tugging or a prompting, tingles and tears for no reason, and a warmth of knowing there is more, then read on. This is not a light read. It may take once, twice or even three times before an awakening stirs within you. It is written from my soul's perspective experiencing the fullness of multidimensional life as a physical being on Earth.

This wasn't always so. I have come to remember who *I AM*. And through this process my life changed, my vibration shifted, my atomic structure regenerated. I've been led into surrender and the Highest Conscious Self I have ever known (and have actually always been). My journey required my release of every belief system I have ever valued; it dared me to be my God Presence. If this story inspires you and leads you on your way to discovering your soul essence...well, then I have served my calling.

Prior to my journey to Lake Louise, Chief Joseph related to me in a message: *"The seeds you planted on your stargate pilgrimage become harvest through the words of Wisdom that you weave."* This is the harvest story. It is a powerful warp and weft of Light grids intersecting horizontally and vertically opening a passageway through both the Earth and the Spiritual networks. As I learned from Caroline Myss, *"It is very risky to speak on behalf of God...but it is possible to speak with integrity of our own experiences with the God who has come to us individually."* I share with you in these pages my experience with God who has come to me. *Journey OM.*

# Starting Out

Today is July 29, 2009. I've been in Whitefish since mid-July finishing the last edits of *Journey OM, A Soul Journeyer's Adventure*, tending to the garden and awaiting my husband Jim's arrival from San Diego when summer vacation will truly begin. There's not much to do until then but breathe in the mountain air, float on the rippling lake waters, reflect on the last three months and dream of that first heart tugging hug when Jim deplanes.

The Stargate Pilgrimage is months old and quickly fading in my memory. Fortunately, remembrances are preserved on paper. Good thing. Already my mind is playing tricks with me. Having finished the last pages, I am ready to tie a virtual ribbon around the completed manuscript and hand it over to Archangel Gabriel. As a closing ceremony, I complete the incredible adventure as it began, joining in meditation with Chief Joseph and the other ascended beings who journeyed alongside me.

The separation of time, space and dimension dissolves and we unite as one in the etheric realms focusing on the Heart of Truth, the

Mind of Wisdom and the Source of Creation. In quiet anticipation, I await the Ascended Masters—Chief Joseph along with Lord Sananda holding the energy of the Christ consciousness; Lord Maitreya and Lady Nada. Buddha appears representing the Wisdom of Enlightenment which is showering the planet. It is a gathering of all the Ascended Masters of Wisdom. We are on an enormous etheric conference call today with the guides and masters who will assist Scout and me on our next adventure.

This ceremony will seed my consciousness with keys and concepts of the Universe. I am about to discover that I will take a trip to Lake Louise. The Ascended Masters will direct me on my quest and show me the way.

Chief Joseph speaks:

*Shima, you are a pioneer, star seed, warrior and ascension master. You have said, 'Thy Will Be Done' and so through you we are guiding the star systems and leading the star treks for others to complete their final destiny. As an ascension master you journey for the sake of the people. On your Journey OM pilgrimage you entered eternity, timelessness, a moment without time. You brought the past from 10,000 years ago, from 1877 to the present, and from this present moment you will open the doorway to the eighth sacred stargate called the Ascension Gate. The path of my prophecy you have just completed has taken you on a cycle of planting to harvest to the deep space of winter retreat. The harvest moon begins the gathering of the gifts from sacred Earth to nourish the people through the deep times of winter when Earth enters silence. The winter moon will soon follow the harvest moon. The seeds you planted on your pilgrimage become the harvest through the words of Wisdom which you weave. Your destiny as a journeyer has been quite exquisite. Even we struggle to put into language the multiple Universes you experienced and how distantly your essence was created. And so dear one you have been a journeyer since the beginning of no time and the continuation of eternity.*

*You were destined to fulfill my prophecy and now complete, you enter this time when you rest upon the spirit of your journey. This is spiritual food in this time of winter. In the way of days gone by when we gathered food in Autumn; when the Earth no longer gave us living green fruits and the game was scarce we had plenty to eat. This is a time for you to know your soul's journey and your inner connections to the deep, deep energy of your Spirit Lodge, the Temple of God that is now descended in your physical form.*

*This pilgrimage you have made is a spiritual gift opening up for you and others pathways and places you now have eyes to see and the Wisdom and understanding to know. You now have an acute sense of perception, Wisdom and vision. The keen senses you invoked on your journey are the senses now allowing you the special sight, the special hearing, the special knowing to see other trails, journeys and promises. You have received the gift of clairaudience, the voice telling you exactly what the next step is. This is the language of God. This is the time for the Way of Peace on your ascension path.*

*In the old days when we journeyed into new land there was always a 'seer' who would give counsel to the tribal leaders.*

*When we made choices from Wisdom in balance with Mother Earth we would flourish. When our choices were made from a sense of fear the rivers dried up and food became scarce. The seer did not have to walk the unknown country to tell us what we needed to know. This higher consciousness is the unknown country of which the seer spoke. We as a people in 1877 could not go to this Ascension Gate because we lived in the world of survival, protection and refuge. The seer foretold that when survival is no longer our focus and the way of Peace is at hand someone will lead the people to the eighth stargate, to the Ascension Gate. You, Shima, live in a world of Grace and you know this. You will make a pilgrimage to Lake Louise and will open the eighth sacred place, the place I could not go.*

*All of the many Star Nation Chiefs and Native Ancestors will join you. Call to the Masters of Wisdom, the Ascended Masters, all the angels and many guides and ask that all of the Ancestors of Turtle Island hear your voice. Ask for them to make this pilgrimage with you and journey on behalf of my people who never crossed the border and for those who did—Chief White Bird with his people the Nez Perce, Sitting Bull of the Sioux and Crazy Horse of the Lakota. Even those who made it to Canada could not open the Ascension Gate for they traveled for refuge; for food and safety. They traveled for protection and for survival. It was not time.*

*Announce to them that Chief Joseph is walking by your side. I will travel with you on these sacred days to the place I was going when I was stopped. Multitudes of Spirits and Ancestors will stand in a great ring of Light. This is the action of prophecy. I,*

*Chief Joseph ask you to fulfill the prophecy I was not able to finish.
I will be with you when you do this. Your journey will be well and
fruitful. August 8, 2009 is the day. Aho. I have spoken.*

## THE SEED IS PLANTED

Months earlier Jim and I planned a summer trip to Lake Louise.
Is this why we were going? For none of the reasons we thought?
Last summer I had traveled with a friend to this majestic place in
Canada and I couldn't wait to return and share the beauty with my
beloved. But this is a trek only to be made in warm weather so we
waited patiently for the cycle of the seasons and the return of summer. This trip of prophecy to Lake Louise had been put in motion
long before my knowing, similar to the beginning of the stargate pilgrimage last May when our departure was disguised as travel to
Spokane for car repairs. All I had to do was say *Yes.* Chief Joseph
and the Ascended Masters had taken care of everything else.

*During the period of my exodus I prepared the way of the seven
stargates. In my lifetime I never made it to this sacred lake in
Canada but that is where I was headed when I was stopped at
Bear's Paw in Montana. I was stopped because the time was not
right. The time is NOW. You are to open the way of the eighth
stargate at Lake Louise on this day of August eighth.*

*This is a heart journey. Prepare for your journey through the heart with your family and those you love. You will journey to the source of ascension through the heart to open the gate I could not open. In your heart, enter sacred space and see yourself standing at the seventh stargate at Bear's Paw. Visualize an imaginary line in a soft curve weaving the path of radiance from Bear's Paw to Lake Louise. This is where you will find and open the eighth stargate. This pathway of light will illuminate your way. It is the time of ascension and the Way of Peace. The time to open the Ascension Gate is NOW.*

*The activation of the stargates on the pilgrimage you just completed opened an ascension pathway for all of humanity to ascend. This is the gateway of infinity which takes the whole of Mother Gaia into the ascension realm, allowing all Earth to ascend. It is a pathway which takes us into new dimensions and higher consciousness; a land which humans have never journeyed. This is the opening of ascension energy for the planet through the ray of Sananda. The eighth stargate stands alone. It needs no support for it is gifted with more Light than any other portal up to this time. It will not close. It will not recede. It will constantly open wider and wider. Each pilgrim that goes through allows the portal to increase its magnitude. This is the infinity journey. It is the place where people go beyond choices of survival into internalizing Grace. This is the cosmos and this is Earth.*

*There are many gifts yet to come to Earth from the cosmos and the Star Nations; Wisdom from the Ancients and the ones of the future. This eighth stargate will be the source of cosmic Wisdom for Earth; a source of Peace; a source of Grace; a source of Oneness and balance. The heart ray, the ascension ray of Lord Sananda will illuminate the eighth stargate. And as Lord Sananda's ray enters Earth it will be a source of stability calming the birthing Mother Gaia that her ascension may be gentle and delightful. Your opening this stargate is the privilege and honor of your past soul's acceptance of the journeys you have taken. Blessings be to you in your advancement in the knowledge of the Universe. Aho. I, Chief Joseph have spoken.*

I received Chief Joseph's message through an open heart. Enlightened with his Wisdom we were ready to embark on our adventure to Canada.

## BACKING UP

This journey really began in April 2009. For those of you who just happened upon this book let me back up. The story of the stargate pilgrimage on the Chief Joseph Trail is a once upon a time adventure: once upon a time 10,000 years ago; once upon a time in 1877; and once upon a time in May 2009. It is the true story of the ten day pilgrimage Scout and I took at the behest of Chief Joseph to complete his destiny. Everything actually happened to me and Scout. We experienced supernatural encounters, unveiled divine revelations and confronted forces of darkness as we retraced Chief Joseph's journey through Oregon, Idaho, Wyoming and Montana— a twelve hundred mile trip. What began one hundred thirty-two years ago ended in 2009 with the fulfillment of the Chief's prophecy. Along the way we discovered the stargates seeded by Chief Joseph linking the Pleiades and the Chief Joseph Trail to spiritual lessons, Light codes and Universal Truth destined to be revealed.

Who were the Nez Perce in 1877? Or in their native language, who were the Nimiipuu? My research revealed the Nez Perce were a prosperous people, a healthy group standing well over six feet tall when the average height at that time was five feet six inches. Long before women's rights were recognized the Nez Perce respected and revered their women. The women were rightful property owners of lodges, food sources and wares which they freely bought and sold for their own profit. If not treated with honor, a woman could choose to leave a relationship without prejudice or reprisal from the community. Most interestingly, the Nez Perce accepted intermarriage between other tribes. The family and relatives of the outside tribe would become family of the Nez Perce. In this way, all were their brothers' keepers.

The Nez Perce revered beauty. They were renowned for their skilled beadwork and their handiwork was prized among all nations. They were savvy businessmen, ranchers and ingenious inventors. They were recognized as the finest breeders of the Appaloosa and their stock was sought for its speed and stamina.

The white settlers looked down upon the Nez Perce, calling them nomads. In fact, they were masters of the land and its resources, moving to the warmth and shelter of the canyons in the long, cold winter months, summering in the meadows and following the migration of salmon and buffalo for year round sustenance. The Nez Perce were people of open minds and open hearts. They embraced the new, welcoming settlers from the east to homestead on their land and share their bounty. Sadly, the American settlers and the cavalry did not hold the same values and ideals. In the end they took what the Nez Perce honored as gifts from the Creator to be enjoyed by all. Even though the cultural battle was lost, Peace prevailed; ahead of even our time, the Nez Perce lived beyond the illusion of separation, believing in Oneness, Peace, Love and Harmony. Their Pleiadian star lineage ran close to the surface. And now, we too, are finally awakening to this realization.

## AMAZING AFFIRMATION—ANCIENT ASTRONAUTS

If there were any doubt left to dispel before embarking on this pilgrimage, the most amazing affirmation came, from of all places, the television. One night while Jim was surfing TV stations he came upon the History Channel and a documentary called *Ancient Astronauts*, a show discussing the probability and evidence of extraterrestrial life on Earth. Thinking it would interest me, he recorded it. A few days later I sat down to watch. Halfway through the program there was mention of the Pleiades and the graphic display of the Seven Sisters constellation. I perked up. Interesting, I thought. Hmmm, I wonder…

I placed the show on pause, grabbed Jim, searched for a piece of paper and marker and began to trace the outline of the constellation. Jim, shaking his head, wasn't following my line of thinking. Reducing the outline to fit the size of my haphazard stargate map, I over-laid the constellation outline onto the seven travel sites I had identified on the Chief Joseph Trail. We looked at each other in absolute amazement. The stars and sites matched! Each one of the Seven Sisters stars aligned perfectly to a potential stargate site I had marked on the map. No longer could we think this pilgrimage was something I'd made up for fun. We had just been shown the location of the stargates in a very graphic way. This was indeed God work! Guidance from the Ascended Masters and what could only be revealed in my heart through Faith and Trust led me to the stargates.

Preparation for this journey required an intense physical recalibration and several spiritual initiations in order to hold the vibratory frequency required. Before we departed, it was necessary to enhance my sensitivity to geomagnetic fields so I could find the stargates. The second download brought in seven Light packets, or rays, from the cosmic Christ through the Pleiadian Councils of Light. These rays would be projected from my energy body to trigger the activation points in the stargates. Finally, I was asked to undergo an initiation by Lord Melchizedek—a most sacred honor enabling the bridging of the highest Source energy we can presently access with the third dimension vibrations of Earth. The initiations were most intense. I did not sleep for seven days. All of my senses were heightened. I wrote, studied and prepared non-stop with great clarity. Once this new frequency was fully integrated I rested. With my body prepared and the job offer accepted, we were ready to embark.

Ten days and 4,300 miles later we returned to where we began—Whitefish Lake. A message from Chief Joseph awaited me.

*Shima, it is I, Joseph who speaks to you now. At the activation of each stargate an Ancient Star-Chief was awakened and journeyed with you on your pilgrimage pathway. These Chiefs awaken the creation energies mirrored from the Stars to Earth and from the Earth to the Heavens. They have now emerged from the seven sacred stargates and at Bear's Paw, the stargate you call Ascended Earth. These seven Ancient Star Chiefs rejoined me to form an Alliance of Peace in the cosmic order and on the earthly plane. What transpired in the spirit realm is mirrored at the seventh stargate.*

*There are rivers of life which will flow on the Earth that were dried up, rivers of life that will flow from the Ascension Gate seeding the body of Mother Earth with sacred life force. From the Mothers of the Ancients and the Cosmic Councils, the Mothers' milk will flow through the rivers of life feeding the spirits waiting for this gift to awaken.*

*You have come full cycle. This all has come to be in the passing of time which is infinite and immortal. The Ascension Gate lives for all time in the Heart of Turtle Island, in the Heart of Mother Earth, in the Heart of the Divine Mother's Light, the Heart of Creation. I AM Joseph. I AM your brother. Aho. I have spoken.*

That journey ended as all journeys do. We were complete—or so we thought. I sat waiting for the next tap on the shoulder. It came quickly on the heels of our return. Our work was not done; Chief Joseph's destiny not yet complete. "*NOW is the time of ascension and the Way of Peace. The time to open the Ascension Gate is NOW—August 8, 2009 is the day.*

The story you are about to read is the second of the *Journey OM* series. On our mission in 2009 to open stargates seeded by Chief Joseph in 1877, our consciousness was expanded and our reality of who we were as Shima and Scout was forever changed.

Trailhead to Dolphin's Halo, the first stargate on the Chief Joseph pilgrimage

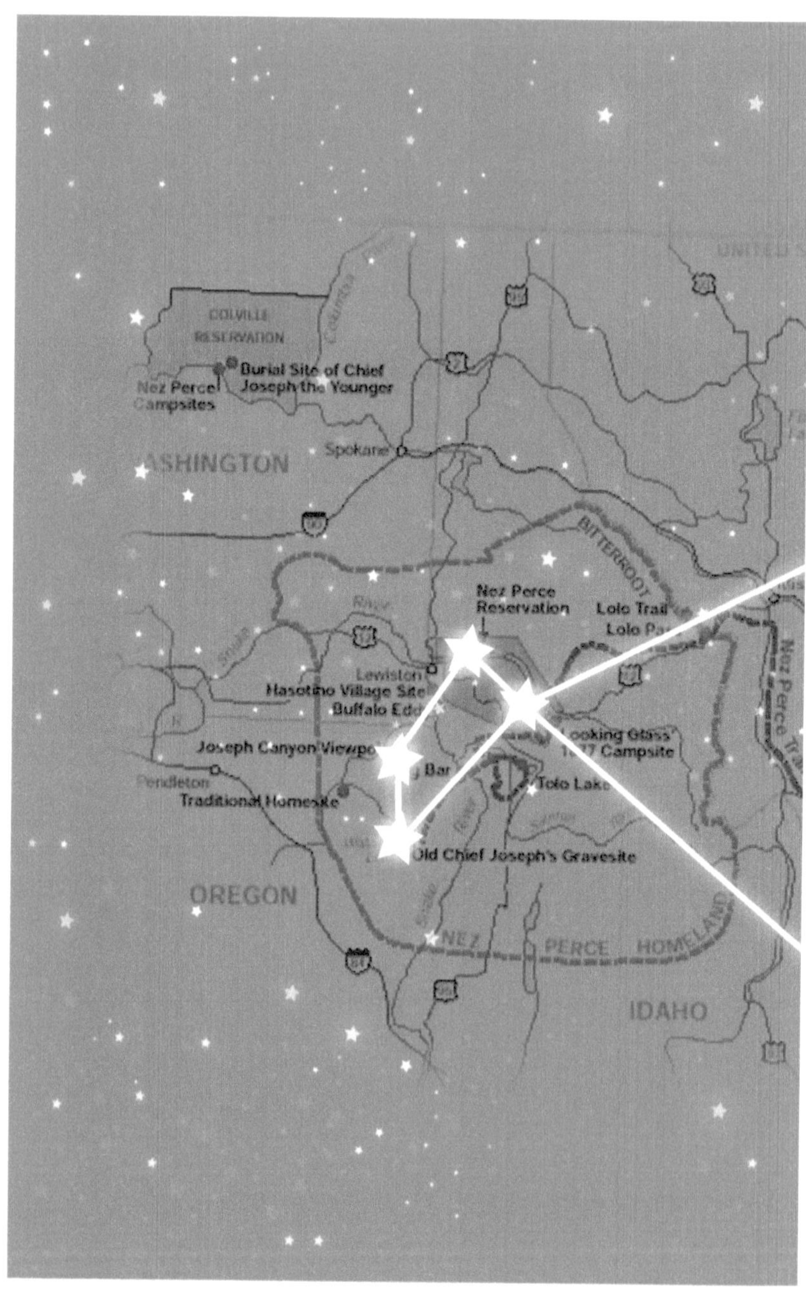
COLVILLE
RESERVATION
Burial Site of Chief
Joseph the Younger
Nez Perce
Campsites
WASHINGTON
Spokane
Columbia
BITTERROOT
Nez Perce
Reservation
Lolo Trail
Lolo Pass
Nez Perce Trail
Lewiston
Hasotino Village Site
Buffalo Eddy
Looking Glass'
1877 Campsite
Joseph Canyon Viewpoint
Bar
Tolo Lake
Pendleton
Traditional Homesite
Old Chief Joseph's Gravesite
OREGON
NEZ
PERCE HOMELAND
IDAHO
UNITED S

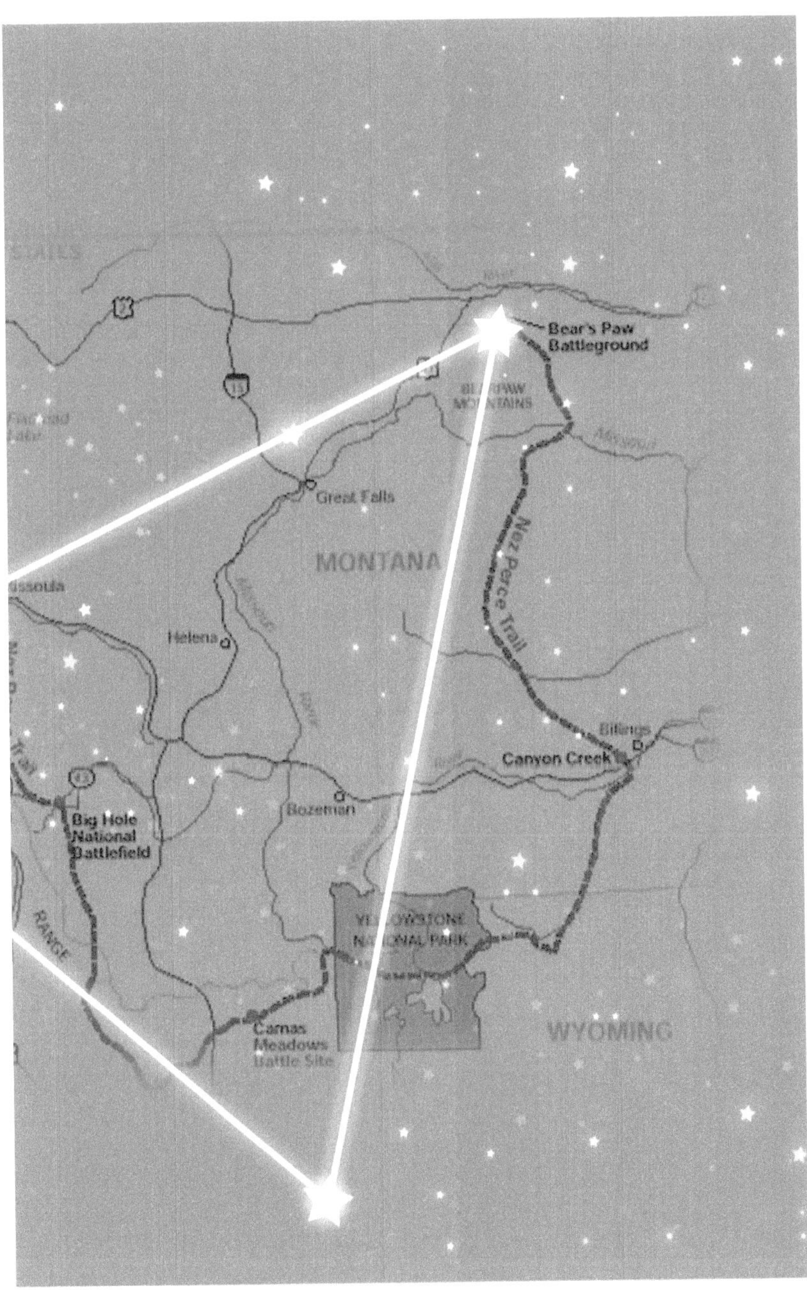
Bear's Paw
Battleground
BEAR PAW
MOUNTAINS
Missouri
Flathead
Lake
Great Falls
MONTANA
Nez Perce Trail
Missoula
Helena
Billings
Canyon Creek
Big Hole
National
Battlefield
Bozeman
RANGE
YELLOWSTONE
NATIONAL PARK
Camas
Meadows
Battle Site
WYOMING

# $J$ULY 29

## $S$HIMA IN $W$HITEFISH

It had only been two months since we'd traveled Chief Joseph's Trail, reliving the hopes, the fears, the faith and the conviction which spurred this group of peaceful warriors in 1877. For us this journey was to be a different reality. Ours was not a flight of loss and hopelessness and injustice. It was a trail of illumination and an awakening to who we truly are. Ours was a pathway of ascension guided by the Ascended Masters. The purpose of our pilgrimage was to dispel disillusion and awaken the 5th dimensional Pleiadian consciousness of Peace, dormant 10,000 years, waiting for this moment of revival.

The path of Chief Joseph was much more than an ascension path for planet Earth. As difficult as it may be to understand, we opened the flow of harmony and wove pathways of Light and Peace into many other dimensions and planes of energy. We linked the cosmic forces of the Seven Sisters Constellation and Mother Earth, attuning not only mankind but also the Pleiadians to the continuum of Light and Peace. Mother Earth is one of many other planets, star systems and their inhabitants in the process of ascension. What we transformed and transcended on Earth by opening the stargates on Chief Joseph's Trail we also transformed and transcended on the Pleiades. Every Universe is comprised of many dimensions and every dimension holds sub-dimensional fields, planes, timelines and parallel realities. Everything on the macrocosm is mirrored in the microcosm.

Consider that our bodies are comprised of billions and trillions of cells, zillions of molecules and atomic and sub-atomic particles too numerous to count, each formed from the same substance—carbon, silica, water and iron for example—yet unique to itself by the velocity of its specific vibration. When in energetic harmony with one another these unique molecular patterns can unite to create different organs and systems. The combination of these individual molecular patterns creates the composite human body. The human body and its different organs and systems is similar to the Universe and its many dimensions, sub-dimensions and planes, all combining to make up the greater Universe. Think of the vibration of silica in our body beginning to resonate to the frequency of silica quartz crystals growing beneath the surface of Earth which in turn tunes into the molecular vibration of silica sand covering our beaches and ocean beds. As we hone into nature in this example, through quartz crystal we discover our natural tone. The macrocosm is the microcosm. It is all energy taking on different forms, but ultimately all one. "We are all One" continues to deepen, reminding me home.

The Pleiades comprise many dimensions and realms at differing stages of evolvement. The collective consciousness on the second dimension of Pleiades experiences duality and separation similar to our collective experience of duality on Earth. On our first stargate pilgrimage we confronted darkness and duality at Broken Sequence, Souls Knolls and the Heart of the Monster, each mirroring the darkness and duality of the Pleiadian second realm. When we ultimately transmuted this negative energy both Earth and Pleaides were redeemed.

The galactic misuse of power is troubling to me. Lower forms of galactic energy engage in power struggles affecting the control and manipulation of the ruling structures of our planetary political systems. Chief Joseph understood the greater vision and knew that the harmony in the heavens affects the earthly planes and vice versa. His ascension pathway created the opportunity and the capacity to access lower galactic realms and transmute the mis-qualified use of power which was negatively impacting both our evolution on Earth and the Pleiadians.

# *Then and Now*

One hundred thirty-two years ago the misconceived reality of the Nez Perce exodus was a quest for Peace. History inscribed its course of death, destruction and hatred on the land and its people and marked us, the future generations of Americans, guilty as the children of their oppressors. We can now see that all is in perfect and divine order and know that there is more to be seen of these historical events than the depiction of a dismal journey. Back then it was a story of struggle, survival and surrender fraught with spiritual lessons to be shared and learned at the harsh hand of the heartless for our benefit.

It is time to shed the Nez Perce story of this trail of tears with new Light. Like all Native American lore and tradition, the ancient Wisdom of the Elders is kept alive through storytelling, passed down to our children. This is what I've been asked to do and why I share with you, material written from glimpses I perceive in this moment. It will stand the test of time because it is pure of Heart and intention—it is my Truth. And in time, another teacher will come along and expand on my glimpse of God's infinite Universe.

## THE NEZ PERCE—FIGHT OR FLIGHT

It was not an easy relationship between the chiefs on the Nez Perce exodus in 1877. The chiefs banded together, leaders united by a common threat, but they were chiefs of their own tribes with unique traditions, distinctive leadership styles and opposing opinions as to how to face their foe. On this exodus the chiefs were bound by lineage, but not necessarily by agreement. The elders and former chiefs did not want to fight the white man any longer—their numbers were too many, the threat of loss too great. Their choice was to abandon their homeland and start anew in Canada, King George's land of the Old Woman. Some warriors wished to remain and fight, to drive the white man from their land and to reclaim what was rightfully theirs. These young warriors of the Chief White Bird and Chief Looking Glass clans sought revenge and were impulsive in their actions. This small group of warriors and their misguided zeal sealed a fate none had bargained for.

Chief Joseph had not supported this *fight or flight* approach and had not anticipated the killings. He wanted Peace. Initially, he repeatedly called to the other chiefs to turn back to their own country while they still could. But as the trek took its toll and remaining on their homeland became a desperate option, Joseph's counsel seemed the only voice of Wisdom. His was a steady hand and a calming influence, assuring the orphaned children were clothed and fed and elders made comfortable and warm. Chief Joseph only wanted solace for the broken bodies and weary spirits of his people. He had no patience for hateful hearts and fierce pride.

The bands disagreed over the young warriors' actions. They differed on the constant push and drive that could not be maintained by the children, the elderly and the weak. Chief White Bird, Chief Looking Glass and Chief Joseph joined together as best they could to bring their people to safety, but the undercurrent of differing strategies simmered. Because they were brothers in honor and respect they conceded to one another, but nothing felt right to any of them. In the end it was a thoughtless insult by a young maiden to a proud young brave named Wahlitits that unleashed the chain reaction and long harbored resentment for their suffering at the hands of the white man. As Joseph's destiny would have it, he was away from camp caring for his wife when the tide of emotion swelled to the violence which led to the Nez Perce surrender at Bear's Paw. What was started in his absence became his destiny to fulfill. "Hear me my chiefs, I am tired. My heart is sick and sad. From where the sun now stands I will fight no more. Forever!"

Unable to fulfill his destiny, I am the understudy called upon and agreeing to take the final steps on Joseph's journey. Opening the eighth stargate, *The Ascension Gate,* will once again unite Mother Earth to her celestial family. The surrender of Chief Joseph at Bear's Paw on October 5, 1877 stilled his soul journey. Unable to complete his prophecy to seed the eighth stargate at Lake Louise, Canada, Chief Joseph's destiny remained dormant and incomplete.

At the point of surrender Chief Joseph could not bear to see his wounded men and women suffer any longer. The promise made in exchange for surrender was his people's return to their homeland the following spring. Until then they would go to Tongue River to wait out the winter. This was the first in the sequence of broken promises. Instead they were carted to Bismarck, North Dakota and forced to relinquish 1,100 of their horses—the lifeblood to their independence. As prisoners of war they were moved to the lowlands of Fort Leavenworth, Kansas where water was undrinkable and sickness rampant. They were moved again to Baxter Springs, Kansas and stripped of their lodges and medicine. Finally they were shuttled to northeastern Oklahoma where their numbers continued to diminish. In all over seventy people died from the squalid conditions.

At this juncture Chief Joseph's earthly journey diverged from his soul destiny. In his waning years he remained the voice of Peace, never wavering from his message that ALL people be ONE people. He was granted permission to visit Washington and speak to President Rutherford Hayes and an assembly of officials. From his heart Chief Joseph spoke:

*I cannot understand why so many chiefs are allowed to talk so many different ways and promise so many different things. It makes my heart sick when I remember all the good words and all the broken promises. Good words do not last long. They will not make good the promise of your War Chief, General Miles. I only ask to be treated as all other men are treated. My heart is heavy. We ask that the same law shall work alike on all men. When the white man treats the Indian as they treat each other then we shall have no more wars. We shall all be like brothers, of one father and one mother with one sky above us and one country around us. That all people may be one people; send rain to wash the face of the Earth. Let us put our minds together and see what future we can make for our children. Aho. I have spoken.*

His words fell on deaf ears and the Idaho settlers successfully lobbied to continue their exile. On September 21, 1904, according to his physician, Chief Joseph died of a broken heart.

When cast in balance with nature, all seeds will sprout. We begin at Lake Louise by picking up the trail where Chief Joseph left off, to fulfill his prophecy of Peace and Freedom and open the eighth stargate, the *Ascension Gate*. My mind is spinning. My heart is pounding. The process of moving from the knowledge of the mind to the Wisdom of the Heart has begun. I must get my mind out of the way so my heart can open to the divine Wisdom waiting to unfold. The seeding has begun.

# THE CLARK FAMILY

*This is a heart journey. You will prepare for your journey through the heart with those you love, your family.*

The Clark family—my sisters, brothers, in-laws, nephews and nieces, sons and daughters—will arrive in Whitefish in a few days. We will spend three days hosting family then Jim and I will excuse ourselves away for romantic alone time in Canada—the perfect balance.

Our family reunions are a time when past and present merge, each sibling reliving their personal joys and sorrows of growing up in the Clark family tribe. Each and every year is no different. Some carry wounds that are still bleeding. Others drown their sorrows in wine. Catharsis and recrimination surface perhaps unbidden, but not unexpectedly. With apprehension, each of us awaits the next re-enactment of prior family dramas. What malady of forty years ago will be relived in this reunion? Who will be the one this time to bring up misdeeds to be rehashed? Growing up in the same family, we each lived our separate reality. Over the years the stories take on new meaning, the abuses become abhorrent, and the joys more jubilant. "Remember when?" And the stories begin. Replay. Hit rewind. Replay again.

Jim and I have strategically planned a trip to Canada to shorten this family regression. Time in the towering Canadian Rockies and the depths of turquoise blue water will erase the old family tapes once again revived. Little did I know this journey through the heart with my Clark family tribe was preparing me for another heart journey to Lake Louise, this one orchestrated by God. In Chief Joseph's message I am reminded of this upcoming reunion and the necessary preparation required for opening the *Ascension Gate: This is a heart journey. You will journey to the source of ascension through the heart with your family to open the gate I could not open.*

A few months ago I experienced a "piercing of the heart." It was preparing my way. There are stories in the Bible of Jesus and the pierced heart. Piercing the heart is when any and all forms of wounding are revealed as anti-God matter. Once exposed, they can be released; this was my release of the last held wounds of my heart. I resurrected every aspect of my heart chamber ever closed to eternal Love through all time.

As an initiation through darkness it is most difficult. Piercing the heart and bringing me into total self-Love could only be accomplished through feelings in my emotional body. It can never be completed through the intellectual aspect of the mind. An emotional trigger is required. Translation: anger, abandonment, irritation, resentment, self-reproach, unworthiness and loss—all those ungodly emotions I prefer to think I have transcended. It is about reclaiming soul fragments which were abandoned and bringing them back into the womb of the divine Mother.

Thankfully, we no longer need to learn through darkness, suffering and struggle. How I wish I'd known! That is the misguided means by which many of us in the past chose how to learn; through the vortex of descended energy, the shadow and duality which are in opposition to the Father. This form of learning is no longer necessary. Once I surrendered to the piercing of the heart it became a celebration of the purity of my heart uniting with the white flame.

## REINCARNATION—CREATING LIFE'S STORY

Somewhere in my reading and studies I pieced together my understanding of incarnation as a way of making sense of relationships in my life and the circumstances of my being. A thread here, a revelation there, and the fabric of awareness evolved. Primarily, this interpretation helped me move from intolerance to acceptance. And then a bit more understanding unfolded opening me to compassion and ultimately unconditional Love for those in my life. This story was especially meaningful to help me understand those who are most difficult. Now they are the ones I love and appreciate the most for their selfless service to me. My eyes have been opened to see God in everyone and with new insight Peace has became my soul companion.

We are all sparks of God's magnificent creation, each individually sparked on a specific Ray that collectively carries a unique God quality. We can think of our soul family as those of us who originate on the same Ray and have been together eternally in the non-dimensional Universe. Sometimes we incarnate together in this third dimensional space-time continuum on Earth. Other times members of our soul family remain in other dimensions to assist us on our Earth journey from afar. As soul family members we move in and out of each others' lifetimes depending on what we've been asked and agreed to do to help each other on our spiritual path to enlightenment. Oftentimes when we seek our twin-flame or our soul mate on this physical plane it simply isn't possible. They have chosen to remain off planet where they can better assist us in our ascension process.

Consider each lifetime as a theatrical production. Every actor plays a part for the story to be told and the lessons of each divine Ray to be derived and mastered. Before we incarnate we meet with members of our family of origin for the casting call. My soul lineage is Elohim Peace and the first Ray, through the lineage of Master El Morya, the Elohim Hercules and Amazonia, as well as Archangels Michael and Faith. I am sparked of the first Ray, expressing the God qualities of the Will of God through the power of the Father, omnipotence, protection and Faith. This is where I connect with other first Ray family members. It is from this group that the casting call went out for my lifetime as Darcy and now Shima to help me master the God qualities of the sixth Ray.

Ascension is the mastery of all of the divine Rays. Each incarnation we choose a Ray to master in that lifetime. This lifetime I have chosen the sixth Ray. Even though I originate from the first Ray, Elohim Peace is teaching me Wisdom and Love through the sixth

Ray. I asked for my life lessons and the relationships in my life to out-picture the purity of the Love of Christ and the selfless service of God through spiritual worship and devotion. And so with the intention of mastering the God virtues of the sixth Ray I met with my soul family members who were not already engaged in a lifetime and were free to reincarnate with me.

We create a storyline together determining our race and ethnicity and the geographic location where we will live. Every detail of our life story is laid out for this upcoming Earth drama, all geared to create lessons that will awaken us to our pure God Essence and increase our Light quotient to become the purest expression of Love. Character by character the actors are cast.

Two members wish to learn unconditional Love. I volunteer:

"I will play your daughter, Darcy. I will rebel against all you believe in. I will cause you endless pain and frustration. I will push every button, driving you to your limits so the last thing you feel is love. In this way you can learn tolerance, allowance and ultimately unconditional Love. It will not be easy to be such a rebel child but I will volunteer for this role because of my pure Love for you."

And two of my beloved soul family step up and say:

"We'll play the part of your father and mother to teach you what you desire to learn. We will be committed to your enlightenment and if you do not learn through Love and subtlety we will ratchet up the lessons. We will do whatever it takes until you master what you truly desire. We will do this because we love you so much. It will not be easy for us to play this part for we may at times appear to be cruel and unloving. But we will do it for you: Gift Given. And in return we will master the third divine Ray of cosmic Love. Gift Received."

And so the roles of father, mother and daughter are selected. One by one each character is cast. With this parable I could imagine everyone in my life volunteering for a role to help me on my path to enlightenment, and me helping them on theirs. In this way I could detach from their annoyances, abuses and attacks. I could see the Love behind their motives. I could forgive myself for my seemingly unloving behavior. This is how I've learned the mastery of the seven sacred Flames lifetime after lifetime and how I have provided Love and service to my soul family. Gift Given; Gift Received.

After this *performance* is over we join again as our pure God Presence, taking off the costumes we wore. This is when we all sit backstage and have a good laugh.

"Boy, did I really play that part to the hilt!"

"Yes you did. And I'm not sure you had to go so far!"

We review. And we remember who we truly are. And we Love. No forgiveness necessary. The gifts were wrapped in disguise. Those who chose to be the loving ones in our life, the peacemakers and the providers of security, the teachers and the lovers, theirs was the easy job—the beloved heroes and heroines. It's the ones who volunteered for the harsh parts of this theatric for whom we should be most thankful—the mother who has no time for us, the ridiculing sisters and the competitive brothers, the absent father, the abusive boss, the neglected children, the aloof husband and the unhappy wife. You know them in your own life, each playing a different role, not truly who they are. These are the ones who in their selfless way disregarded their pure God Essence of Love to be our teachers and serve each of us on our path.

As we move back into the Golden Era and the higher consciousness of pure Love, Peace and Harmony we no longer have to choose to learn from suffering and pain, loss and scarcity. This is a misconception we chose to create. It is not necessary. We can just as easily learn from Love and Grace, and Kindness. We can meet in this dimension or beyond as whom we truly are, God Beings, wearing no masks, no costumes, no illusions, no made-up storylines—God to God loving each other on our way.

# WEDNESDAY, AUGUST 5

## THE OBSERVER

Time is illusive. On Chief Joseph's stargate pilgrimage I had one month to prepare. This leg of the journey I have less than a week.

The fuels firing the family reunion are smoldering. As the observer it had been delightful. I had not been drawn into the drama, the stories or the judgments. I sat in joy in my family's company as if I were among the Ascended Masters.

I first became aware of this new gift of being the observer last January when Jim had been "auctioned off" as a celebrity chef for a charity fundraiser. The winning bidders were an homogenous mix: a right-wing radio talk show host and his scripted wife, a charming, bow-tied weatherman on the local conservative TV station, three naval officers from the Viet Nam era and their patriotic wives—all in the good company of Rush Limbaugh. President Obama had just been elected and the inauguration was quite the buzz.

The dinner crowd was not pleased with this democratic turn of events. Fueled by ever-flowing wine the conversation was prejudiced, political and opinionated. In the past I would have found this situation intolerable. All of my judgments would have boiled to the surface and I would go toe-to-toe debating our differences. This night, however, I witnessed. I observed. I actually enjoyed. For the first time I experienced that I could be anywhere with anyone and hold on to my love for mankind. I had relinquished my beliefs. I understood what the Masters were saying when they talked of being the observer.

Living in Faith has its rewards. There is an observable sequence. The pieces fall in place quicker, remembrance of past events make sense in the present. The stepping stones of understanding are spaced more closely, a step instead of a leap. As time collapses, a life of Faith and Trust, the new life of Heaven on Earth the Ascended Masters foretold, is upon us. Since my return from the initial pilgrimage I can see the synchronicity of events in perfect order and divine timing weaving God's plan for me.

We awaken to a Whitefish mountain morning greeted by a mother deer and her two fawns, a sign of Peace to follow. Deer are wanderers, never twice tracking the same path, always luring us into exploring new adventures, similar to our wanderings along the Chief Joseph Pilgrimage. We have encountered some aggressive negative circumstances over the last three days and now the deer gently guide us to seek out safe and nurturing situations. Their antlers, symbolic of antennae, connect us to higher forms of attunement; just what we need to pick up the frequency which will show us the way.

It's been a tumultuous morning, remnants of the debris of last night's family festivities are still waiting to be dusted off our etheric field. We take time to consciously step through the illusion of spilled tomato juice, splattered bleach and an unhappy sister's scolding for not being on time.

After learning of our trip to Lake Louise, my friend Sean from the Sanctuary in British Columbia, suggested I contact Starwalker, an acquaintance of his who lives in Golden near Lake Louise. As an ascribed guardian of the etheric temple of Archangel Michael, Sean suggested she may be an important link on my journey. I reached out to her via e-mail, hadn't heard back and had forgotten about my query. Now, just before leaving, I checked my e-mail and there was a reply from Starwalker to my earlier message. The tone of her message piqued my intuition; I received her message with hesitation and uncertainty. Meet? Yes? No? I do not reply.

Spills cleaned up and errands complete I sit now in silence, in meditation to begin my journey by connecting with my Master Lord Sananda. A moth caught on the wrong side of the window. I take a moment to free him to the outdoors. A pen out of ink; I stop to refill. Finally a moment of stillness and I immediately feel his presence. The softness, the Peace, soothes my frayed nerves. In this moment I begin to write, tuning in to the language he will speak to me, a language rusty from little use, but so anxious to be revealed.

*It is me, Sananda with Archangel Michael. Take our hand. We will lead you now. Before you begin we will clear you of illusion—family. Not much to do, you weathered well, but the vibration is harsh just the same—the language, the volume, the chaos, the wine. Sit a bit longer with us. Bring in Jim. St. Germain is here with the Violet Flame. The talisman is to come with Jim.*

The talisman! I almost forgot! Although at the time I had unconsciously tried to divert Scout from receiving this spiritual gift, Spirit was tenacious. It found its way to its rightful owner after we had opened the fourth stargate *Heart of the Golden Rose* by the Clearwater River near Kamiah, Idaho. After opening each stargate I am intent on finding a souvenir. Usually a feather, a stone or an interesting piece of wood attracts my attention, a symbol to mark and remind. At *Heart of the Golden Rose* nothing appeared so I cajoled Scout into stopping at a souvenir shop.

Problem was there were none to be found. A run-down, ramshackle smoke shop was the only store in sight. No, I wasn't interested in stopping there, not my kind of place, but Scout encouraged so we pulled in. We walked in announcing our arrival by the jangle of bells attached to the door knob. There was no escaping now. The air was stale with tobacco and any well-intentioned plan to spring clean long past. Cartons of cigarettes lined the walls like movies at Blockbuster. Knick-knacks cluttered the shelves.

The clerk, wizened, old, skinny and wrinkled stood guard. No hellos here. I turned to leave and there by the exit was a small display case. It contained some Indian crafts, nothing much, a few dusty pieces consigned and forgotten. I noticed a small piece of beadwork with an interwoven rose. Having just opened *Heart of the Golden Rose* I perked up. Interesting, but not exciting. It didn't call me. Next to it was a medallion and two matching earrings of finely beaded handwork—tiny amethyst, onyx and white pearls surrounding a golden heart. Two brass feathers hung from the circle.

"You have to have it!" Scout said.

Again my ego stepped in to thwart Spirit's way: "No, too expensive."

Scout passed the money to the clerk and we were out the door before I knew it. The talisman had found its keeper—Scout.

I pause from my meditation to gather Jim's talisman and there beside it is the picture of Archangel Michael. The pieces are beginning to appear. Settling in once again to meditate, I am distracted by the thought: *Prepare to go to Lake O'Hara. If you are to go it will be clear, but first do the homework.* With this internal message I again shift from meditation to surfing the web. God will forever wait. I log on to Starwalker's website for information on Lake O'Hara and begin to print the pages to read and study along the way.

And I print, and print and print—the printer will not stop! It has taken on a life of its own; over and over, page after page of the same. With multiple pages in hand I ask the angels to intercede, hardly in the mindset necessary to tackle technology. The printer has crashed, stuck on Starwalker's website. Why Starwalker and why *her* website to create the crash? It has frozen on this message. An omen? An opportunity for discernment?

On our return, this encounter with Starwalker's website plummets Jim into a technological nightmare taking hours, days, countless geeks and dollars to resolve. With Faith and Trust that all is in divine order and always for the highest good, I do not try to fathom the meaning behind messages. But I do remember responding to the tone of her message with hesitation and uncertainty. My intuition did not want me to miss this signpost. I do not meet Starwalker. *Journey OM.*

We're good to go! Packed up and on the road, we're heading to our first stop, Fairmont Hot Springs. Ooh la la! The anticipation of a rejuvenating soak to cleanse body and spirit in the natural hot springs hurries us along. But it was not to be. Our guides stepped in and we were divinely diverted. When we arrived, Fairmont was crowded and noisy, a stinky, public pool kind of place with too many pee-ple in the pool. Hundreds of tourists, bathers and swimmers of all ages and sizes were jockeying for space—crowds of humanity—no ambiance.

As we walk up to the entrance we are met by a parade of bathers shuffling out in all stages of undress. Thunder, lightning and the lifeguard's whistle had just emptied the pool. A gift. A blessing. We had just been divinely diverted by thunder from the heavens. Onward to Radium Hot Springs, another mineral springs a short drive down the road.

As we drive the skies open and the rains let loose; a downpour from the heavens cleansing and clearing, purifying our way. Radium Hot Springs is a mountain village at the south entrance of the Kootenay National Park. Entering the magnificent Windermere Valley we navigate our way, following the winding Columbia River sided by the sheer cliff walls of the Sinclair Canyon. The Rocky Mountains and the Purcell Mountains cradle the sacred energy as we enter the gateway to what lies ahead on our journey.

When we arrive it is God perfect. Set against the mountainside and surrounded by natural rock walls, the pools are clean, hot and inviting. We've traveled less than 100 miles and the waters of heaven and Earth are playing a big part in our journey. Earlier pummeled by rain, then soaked in the natural mineral waters and shrouded in fog, we are intoning the essence of water into our cellular matrix.

# THE ELEMENTS
# WATER, FIRE, AIR, EARTH

The waters of Mother Earth are the life spring nourishing and sustaining all of her beings. *Water* carries the memory of the divine blueprint from the beginning of creation. It holds the energies of cleansing, communication and emotion. Following the path of least resistance, over time nothing can stop the power of water. Its persistent nature can smooth even the most jagged peaks or carve the deepest canyons. Paradoxically, its gentleness and ease in going with the flow is its source of strength and power.

Numerous times throughout history, land surfaces, including the sinking of Atlantis, were submerged beneath the seas for purification. The Deva of Water is a cosmic star being of pure Source energy moving freely in and out of eternity. She holds the communion between the cosmic star consciousness and Mother Gaia's descended consciousness. She is a cosmic creation coming from the void fertilizing and creating new Universes. The Deva of Water directs our awareness to our similitude with Water. The vibration of Water is as close to the likeness of God/Source as our human mind can absorb. It is by divine design and no mistake that 60% of the male physical body and 55% of the female body are made up of Water, the link to Source and who we truly are.

I am guided to invoke the purifying energy of Water to prepare us for our sacred journey, washing away all of the mis-qualified energies held in our emotional bodies. It encourages our receptivity and opens us to our inter-dimensional selves, resonating to the high frequencies of Peace and Love in every molecule of our being. The rains have cleansed the air and filled it with its vibration. What we are experiencing on a molecular level within our bodies is mirrored in the ethers of Mother Earth.

*As above, so below; as the spirit so the soul; as without so within; and blessed be. So be it and so it is.*

We breathe its essence, we imbibe its beauty and we flow in its fluidity becoming the conduits of Light necessary for what lies ahead. Our energy systems are clear and fluid. We have gracefully and joyfully passed through the first initiation on our *Journey OM.* We allow ourselves to be prepared in this way. Each innocuous event, whether it be a message from the deer, a computer glitch, a rainstorm, or roadside diversion, all has been choreographed. We allow ourselves to be in service by dwelling in the nothingness, free of judgment, expectation and schedule. Water is here to remind us always to be in the flow. There can be no other way. From the West, Neptune and his divine complement Lunara direct the element Water supported by the Undines. The element Water rules the heart and throat chakras. The Waters are crystalline and iridescent and, for those with ears to hear, emit the music of Earth's beautiful atmosphere. As we travel we will encounter the other elements—Fire, Air and Earth—each our teacher, each anxious to share their special qualities for our ascension.

Mother Gaia is a living conscious being, the combined consciousness of all planetary kingdoms who call Earth home. Some of her frequencies are visible and tangible to us, for example, Fire, Air, Earth and Water. Others are more subtle. These elemental forces are vital to maintain every creature on Mother Earth; and we carry the aspects of each element within us. Typically one element is more predominant than the others. Our affinity to a particular element influences our life's design. We are imprinted with the unique patterns and geometries of the elements. It helps define how we perceive life and serves as our personal guide on our path to self-discovery. I am most attuned to Water. My astrological sign is Pisces, a Water sign. When we experience Light through the elements of Fire, Air, Earth and Water we connect to Source. We open to unlimited spiritual power and we discover our unique place in the world.

A cosmic being of each element—Fire, Air, Earth and Water— works together to create a livable and sustainable planet for the angelic beings, humankind and elemental intelligences who call Earth home. Mother Gaia is the embodiment and union of these individual consciousnesses. Each element is directed by a cosmic being and occupies a direction—South, East, North and West. The elemental kingdom, those I think closest to Earth, unlike the angels whom I think of as more celestial, serves under the cosmic beings' direction—all part of the orchestrated Spiritual Hierarchy guided by the Will of God.

Occupying South, *Fire* is the power of transformation and transmutation, a force of extreme purification and change. Its power is ignited in lightning and in the molten core of the planet. The cosmic beings Astrea and Claire are the Elohim of the fourth Ray of Purity. They direct the element of Fire by what is called the Cosmic Blue Lightning or Blue Flame. Their service is to ensure that all of creation, down to the smallest blade of grass, maintains the purity of the divine plan. If you find yourself in distress, you can call on Astrea and Claire and they will release the cosmic circle and sword of Blue Flame shattering all cores of impurity, negativity, or evil—whichever dense energies you may find in your midst. The Blue Flame explodes the center of the energy's destructive forces. After the discord is shattered you can call on St. Germain to transmute the fractured energy with the Violet Flame. This is one way you can create purity in your life.

The elementals under Astrea's and Claire's charge are called the Salamanders. It is easy to view Fire as destructive, but its true gift is in clearing the old and stagnant; creating space for new manifestation and growth. Fire rules the second and third chakras, the centers of creation, manifestation, sexuality and the will.

*Air* is ever present in our breath. It is elusive and intangible and flies under and over the radar of our higher consciousness. Air in the realm of Spirit guides the subtle aspects of our lives; in the world of the mind it can improve our mental acuity and psychic abilities. It is a constant reminder of our soul heritage where we exist as pure Light.

The Air element is governed by Aries and her divine complement Thor. Aries is the cosmic being credited with creating the atmosphere around Earth which softens the radiation of the Sun. Thor governs the actions of the winds, rain and snow which can be as soothing as a spring breeze or as destructive as a hurricane. Thor can move great air-masses to where they are needed most, providing cooling breezes in sweltering heat, filling sails of ships on still seas or directing rain to nourish drought-stricken lands. Under Aries' and Thor's direction the elemental Sylphs purify Earth's atmosphere so we can live. The element Air governs in the direction of East. Air resonates with the third eye and crown chakra.

Virgo, lovingly known as Mother Earth, and her divine complement Pelleur, govern *Earth* in the direction North. Virgo provided the original substance For Earth's elements. If we were to see these elements in their original form they would be something similar to alabaster or white quartz, radiating iridescent colors like a rainbow. The purification and return of the mineral element into light substance is under Virgo's direction. She also nourishes the nature kingdom. What science calls gravitational pull is the actual cohesive power of Pelleur's love and his fully-gathered momentum of centripetal force. Virgo and Pelleur are assisted by the elemental Gnomes. Earth is the energy of life, our life force and the expression of Light manifest in matter. The Earth element represents the most stable and physical aspects of our lives. It vibrates with the root chakra and the Earth Star. The Earth Star chakra supports our connection to life and is the chakra by which we can draw our most enduring power. Earth influences our physical bodies and our ability to manifest material things. When we are grounded to Earth we function day-to-day with ease.

Our bodies and our energies are continually influenced by the vibration of the elements. We are mostly unconscious of their power, but if we tune into their subtle gifts through meditation and practicing mindfulness a new reality opens to us. A simple thought of gratitude for Water's life force causes every atom of hydrogen and oxygen within our body to harmonize with that primordial energy. When we resonate with Fire every electrical spark of energy reacts with Love. Each time we breathe with conscious awareness we invoke the etheric energies and they reply with a deeper connection to Spirit. When we ground ourselves in the beauty of nature Earth gifts us with her Peace and abundance.

Our perpetual dishonor of Mother Earth and our abuse of the elements have caused the elementals to lash out resulting in excessive droughts, flash floods, firestorms, hurricanes, tornadoes and earthquakes. They gather, just as disgruntled human beings do, in certain areas and build up a vortex of unpleasant feelings, thoughts and conversation, which becomes the eye of the hurricane, a flood, a firestorm or other natural disaster creating a track of destruction. Like all of God's creation the elementals at their source are all-loving and all-forgiving and yet throughout the centuries they have built up increasing resentments. Finally they rebel against our lack of gratitude for their service and for our careless and thoughtless pollution of Mother Earth. These natural disasters are not God's creation, but simply mis-qualified energy mis-created by man and the elementals.

Unlike humans however, who have free will, the elementals have limited free will and must answer to our commands. They are forced to take our cue to act out these natural disasters. Through our choice of loving cooperation the elements can assist in the creation of a New Earth. Simply by our awareness of them and our conscious desire to be in harmony with the elemental forces we gain personal strength. More importantly, we empower and strengthen Mother Earth and all of her inhabitants manifesting Heaven on Earth. Gift Given; Gift Received.

Scout and I have been soaked in the natural mineral springs, pummeled by torrents of rain, blanketed by fog, and misted by saturated air particles all in preparation for our calling at Lake Louise. We are in a state of deep relaxation to the sweet point of stillness and oneness as we follow the ribbon of mist outlining the roadway to our next destination, the Deer Lodge Inn at Lake Louise.

We check in to our quarters reminiscent of the early national parks of the 1960s and venture in search of dinner. To our delight the Lodge restaurant, tucked away in the shadow of the Rockies, is a connoisseur's crème de la crème, incredible even to my discriminating chef husband's taste. It has been a long day with a rough start, but in the end, oh so magical. We've arrived on the tails of a beautiful, blustery, Rocky Mountain storm. Every sense soothed and sated. We *Journey OM* in our dreams anxious for the sun to rise.

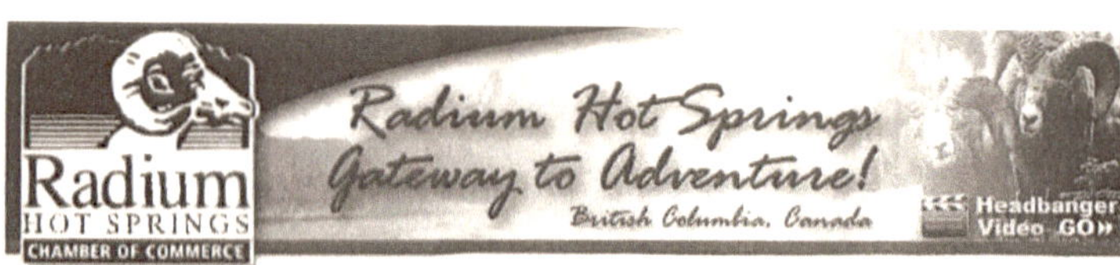


### The Village of Radium Hot Springs
*Home of the World Famous Radium Hot Springs Mineral Pools*

**Radium Hot Springs** is located in BC, Canada with many types of accommodations available, including motels, hotels, resorts, bed & breakfasts, cabins, condos, and RV campgrounds. Located on the "warm side of the Canadian Rockies", **Radium Hot Springs** is British Columbia's best mountain getaway village with unlimited outdoor activities, great dining, golfing, skiing, natural hot spring pools, and the most beautiful alpine scenery you can imagine.

A short 3-hour drive from Calgary, Alberta, at the south entrance of Kootenay National Park, this mountain village has something to please everyone's tastes.

After a leisurely drive through the awe-inspiring Kootenay National Park on the Banff-Windermere Highway, you will encounter the World Famous **Radium Hot Springs Mineral Pools**. These odourless pools are surrounded by natural rock walls, and are guaranteed to soak away your worries and your woes.

Continuing along Highway 93, you will drive between the sheer cliff walls of Sinclair Canyon, entering into the magnificent Windermere Valley. The Village of Radium Hot Springs is located on the Columbia River, between the Rocky Mountain and the Purcell Mountain Ranges.

This small, visitor-friendly community is busy with activities, special events and attractions. Whether it be our championship golf courses, whitewater rafting, hiking, go-carting, fishing, trail riding, mini-golf, shopping or just relaxing in one of our many fine restaurants, you will find all you need to enjoy a fabulous holiday.

If golf is your pleasure, we have 15 courses in the area. Your drive to the courses will range from 3 minutes to 45 minutes.

Radium Hot Springs is only a short drive from Panorama, Fairmont

and Kicking Horse Ski Resorts. Several very popular cross-country skiing trails are featured in the Valley. Our mountains boast some of the finest snowmobiling in the Rockies, with miles of groomed trails and many picturesque backcountry areas are available for the enthusiast.

Big horn sheep, both mule and whitetail deer, bear and elk are seen throughout the Columbia Valley and the National Parks.

The mighty Columbia River flows past the edge of our Village and is bordered by the largest, continuous wetlands in North America. In May of each year there is a bird festival, "Wings Over The Rockies", which attracts bird watchers from around the World.

For those who enjoy beach and water sports, Lake Windermere is a short 20-minute drive south of Radium Hot Springs.

Radium Hot Springs hosts many thousands of visitors throughout the year in all seasons. Come and discover Radium Hot Springs, your gateway to adventure.

We highly recommend a visit to our Chamber of Commerce and Visitor Centre on Main Street East. Our knowledgeable staff will be more than happy to answer any of your questions.

**Passage from my journal—Radium Hot Springs**

NO VACANCY
RESTAURANT
Deer Lodge
PIRAN

Confirmation number: 119473633
Booking date: Jul 12, 2009
Number of rooms: 1
Number of adults: 1
Number of children: 0
Check in: Aug 5, 2009
Check out: ~~Aug 6, 2009~~ 8/9
Total stay: 1 nights

Subtotal: CAD 275.00
Tax: CAD 30.74
Total: CAD 305.74

**Room Information**

Room type: Heritage King
Description: Heritage Room. One King bed, balcony, duvet, coffee maker, complimentary parking and newspaper. No TV. Maximum 2 people.

Daily rate: Taxes and fees are not included. Rates are based on double occupancy.

- Aug 5, 2009 ------ CAD 275.00

Check-in time after 4 p.m. Check-out time before 11 a.m. Rates subject to change. No pets allowed. $25.00 plus GST Cot fee.

Cancellation Policy: Cancel 72 hours prior to arrival to avoid 1 night cancellation or no show charge.

Deposit Policy: All reservations require a valid credit card at the time of booking.

Guarantee Policy: N/A

**Comments and Special Requests**

N/A

**Hotel Information**

Deer Lodge
P.O. Box 100
Lake Louise, Alberta, Canada  T0L 1E0
Map and directions from Calgary

Phone: 403-522-3991

**Passage from my journal—Checking in to the Deer Lodge**

# Thursday, August 6

## Shima and Scout at the Deer Lodge

We awaken to unfamiliar surroundings and take a few moments to get our bearings. Our room is acceptable, but not near the comforts of home. We do our best to rearrange, hiding the knick knacks, bringing in our own down comforter and pillows, incense and essential oils to clear the past energetic presence of others. Inside is not a place to linger. The eternal beauty of the majestic outdoors calls us. Not even the early morning fog can shroud the beauty of this place. As if we had no time to waste we bundle up and hurry outdoors to greet morning at the lake's shore.

It is early, seven-ish. The clouds are low, the air damp and cool, actually beyond cool. I am bundled in several layers. There is stillness by the lake, the kind only to be experienced in the depths of nature. Already it is populated in this early morning hour and the veils of the day are being drawn. Photographers and tripods dot the lakeshore fishing for the perfect shot. Morning is my best time to commune with God, before the chatter of Earth's awakening interferes with my ability to listen. I sit on a rough hewn log bench and like a child who simply can't wait, I put pen to paper—my connection to You—open to receive instructions for our day's adventure. Wisdom and instruction begin flowing to me unobstructed.

*The stargate you will open is a seeding. It will bring the gift of Peace. It will bring individuals into harmonic balance and a state of receptivity so all of their actions can be manifest out of a third dimension reality and into the highest Source level. This is not a constant activation for that would deny free will. Each person must consciously say 'yes' to the gift of this Wisdom. And if they are open to accepting and receiving then the activation point will be ignited and they will automatically tune into the vibration of the Ascension Gate and they will receive all of the gifts that are intended for them.*

*You must consciously choose to receive this gift. It is no longer a function of release but of acceptance. This is not a function of time. It is about spontaneity and your choice to expand into unity consciousness. Simply know all will be given to you in a holy instant at the time of your holy acceptance when there is no separation and all parts of you are redeemed. Know you are the unified consciousness of every aspect of your soul's enlightenment. The gift has always been given. Simply accept the divinity of your perfection and say 'yes.'*

Distracted by the stream of passersby, I pause from pen and paper to reflect on my surroundings. The Fairmont Chateau sits on the shore of Lake Louise. Like a castle reminiscent of times royal, it is a city unto itself. As with all cities, it knows no rest and hums twenty-four hours a day with life-sustaining generators powering the comfort and support of its people. The Fairmont is a global destination; countries, cultures and citizens share equal presence. Colorful country flags billow in the wind while below Swiss costumed bellmen greet arriving guests: *Bonjour, Guten tag, Salaam Alekum, Aloha, Hello.* Cuisine is prepared for every palate regardless of passport. The Fairmont is the perfect expression of unity in diversity—a metropolis in the majestic mountain wilderness.

Two women walk by chirping like birds. Unless keyed into their frequency they are annoying, although once connected to their chatter it is easy to smile. So few cherish the quiet and the sound that comes from no sound; the white space on the page. Therein lay the beauty. I sit among all the people parading by. Just as I look up in this moment of reflection, a swallow flies by, a constant soul companion since meeting at *Swallow's Window,* the third stargate opened in Idaho. The swallow's gift is helping control pesky insects. Here, now, he is letting us know to ignore the pesky people we may meet on our way. Rise above the mundane.

It takes more than this message to sway me. I think, "How can I find my Peace in this multitude of humanity?" *Patience* is the message I hear. Patience—divine timing allowing perfection to manifest—simply balancing our life force energy with Universal Law so we experience each moment as a gift with divine purpose. *Look to the soul of the lake to find your solitude. Look for the Oneness.* This is the message I hear. Oneness—the Ascension Key of Source which births all creation. Creation flows from the vibration of Oneness. Oneness removes any separation, either consciously or unconsciously, hindering the co-creative process. I look to the water and I see my eyes—the color is the same—Oneness. Gift Given; Gift Received.

Our going *in,* entering the space of non-dimensional oneness, was perfunctory yesterday. We've experienced before what to expect and to anticipate what is to come. Impatiently we want it to *just happen.* And yet it is like the diver going deep too fast, too fast and you get the bends. We were advised to depart two days before August 8th in order to calibrate our bodies to the vibration necessary for opening the *Ascension Gate.* It is necessary to be in communion with the land, the lake and the mountains, and more importantly, to find Peace with the energy of the people.

*All will be given to you on your path. Go stripped with as little as you can carry. Then watch for nature, watch for beings who will gift you with each piece you will need along the way. Your journey will be laden with treasures—all to be used in your ceremonies, your rituals, and your story.*

We are vigilant as we watch for signs in nature and for beings— spiritual and earthly—who will gift us with revelations we will need along the way. We have learned that the treasures awaiting us, the signposts and signals only show up in the present moment. We have arrived stripped of expectation, preparation and illusion of what we are here to do. All will come in perfect divine order. At the start, the deer opened the way. There is no mistaking the deer would be an essential guide on our journey. With her acute ability to detect subtle movements and appearances, she teaches the way of gentle Love which will open new doors of adventure for us to wander.

After the soothing gentle Love of the deer, the Water purified us—body and soul. The rain, hot springs, a ribbon of roadway mist, more rain, hail, moist laden air, sky heavy with dew—a total immersion in Water, a cleansing and clearing that left the past behind and opened our senses to the purity found only in the present, unobstructed by thought. We are learning the steps to this choreography of Light and Love. The dance has begun. The world has awakened and the promenade is now crowded with the excitement of tourists beginning their day. We pack up our things and head to breakfast.

Today we will hike to the Plain of Six Glaciers, an eleven kilometer trail with a gain in elevation of 1215 feet at an altitude of 6890 feet. It follows the north shore of Lake Louise passing beneath the quartzite cliffs shadowing the back of the lake, those huge cliffs seen in all the postcards. It is the particles of silt from these cliffs which join the rushing glacial melt-water streaming into the lake that color it with its distinctive turquoise hue. The trail provides views of the terminal moraine left during the Little Ice Age which peaked around 1850. It gradually opens up to reveal six glaciers hanging from the surrounding mountains: Aberdeen, Lefroy, Victoria and Popes Peak. The breathtaking landscape is not the only reward for the hardy. Atop the switchbacks a teahouse welcomes the weary.

Before we set out, we stop in the lobby of the Fairmont. It seems the angels have chosen to greet us and make their presence known in a very audible way. A harpist, attired in costume from the Renaissance era, strums a melody we can hardly believe. This is surely a sign from God. My heart and throat swell along with a knowing that I am receiving another God attunement in preparation for our work ahead. We wait for a song, but the traffic of inquisitive tourists seeking autographs keeps her fingers off her harp. We wait. And then as only the influence of money will do we request a song, Dr. Zhivago's "Somewhere My Love." Tears flow and my breath breaks on sound waves resonating through every cell of my being. So this is what it is to be in the music of angels. She is the Harp Angel.

Lifted on angels' wings we begin our trek to the Plain of Six Glaciers. At the north end of the lake we stop at the headwaters—another tonal water attunement. The waters roar—so much sound there is no sound. Thus far the calibration into the frequency of ascension has been one of water. We bathe in the sound until we are joined by another's voice. Annoyed by the distraction, I pray that further mileage down the trail will distance me from the others. Then I realize this thought has created separation wherein there will be no Peace. Until I can be with the crowds without irritation I will continue to be distracted. I forgive myself. I smile. I pack up and move on not caring if I am among thousands or one.

I've realized there comes a point where *pace* with the people becomes *Peace* with the people. People, too, are part of nature. Somehow I have separated them from the plant, animal and mineral kingdoms, discounting them as nature. Perhaps now, for the first time in lifetimes, I see humankind in its purest form as simply another aspect of the pure beauty of nature, no different than the chipmunks, the deer and swallows in which I take such delight.

The hike is difficult, much more challenging than either Scout or I anticipated. As we focus on our struggle step-by-step in our heavy hiking boots, a young woman with flowing raven hair adorned in henna tattoos comes scampering by—barefoot! We cannot believe our eyes. The trail is rugged and rock strewn. Yet here she is, God's angel dancing up the path! We surrender our heavy footed trodding and the second verse of Waneen WanYan is birthed.

*Do Vah ah Aumm*
*Into the Womb*
*Divine Mother's Birth*
*Ascension on Earth*
*Back to the One*
*Where we've begun*
*Do Vah ah OM*
*Children come home.*

We arrive at the teahouse. Our treat! It is a beehive of activity; we carve out a private setting for ourselves to rest and enjoy our accomplishment before the long hike down. Barely nestled in, we are jostled out of our space by a pushy, loud, intrusive hiker insensitive to her surroundings. Apparently she likes our spot; we surrender to her desires. Peace!

Scout isn't his usual self and our brief rest doesn't seem to help. Another two hours down the long, rocky trail. He is a master at hiding his feelings, physically and emotionally, but this fatigue he can't mask. I think it is the altitude. He carries his discomfort privately, not wanting to affect my balance. We walk the trail retracing our steps in silence. Arriving at the rushing headwaters we stop for a brief respite, allured by a warm hotel room and a steamy-hot bath. The anticipation distracts us away from the present moment, away from the healing waters before us.

We pause and reconnect to the Now, honoring what is here in front of us. Did we really just find ourselves ready to give up this gift in hand, the true healing waters of Mother Gaia for the prospect of chlorinated water delivered through rusted pipes into a porcelain tub? We laugh at our silliness: "the grass is greener, the water purer, and we can negotiate with God." The unending patience God has! And sense of humor! We bless our surroundings with Peace Waters and renew our physical bodies through the currents of sound.

Three days later I discover Scout's distress, evident all over his body, the mark of a spider spelled out in *acute urticaria.* His silence and secrecy cost him days of relief. We all have our lessons to learn—Scout's: All is transparent, there are no secrets. We are our brothers' and sisters' keepers.

## LORD ARCTURUS AND THE ARCTURIAN MASTER HEALERS

The longest of hikes—five hours—and we are tired. I think of Chief Joseph and his valiant people, the wet marches and cold nights stretched out over twelve hundred miles, the four months under threats of the cavalry's bullets with no end in sight. If I could be more tired I become so at the thought of the unfairness of this terrible wrong.

In our hotel room we can take advantage of a soothing bath with Celtic sea salt, Epsom salt and lavender. Chief Joseph's words re-enter my thoughts: *Then the Great Spirit Chief who rules above will smile upon this land and send rain to wash out the bloody spots made by your brothers' hands from the face of the Earth.*

I place the Grandmother Moon Quartz and Aquamarine in the tub. I soak. I relish. I revive, rejuvenate, and refresh. I lay on the bed with my legs and feet raised on three down pillows—simply heaven. Asking Lord Arcturus and the Arcturian healing masters to resurrect me, I immediately feel the buzzing sensation through my body. The carbon to crystalline transformation of my physical body which began in November 2008 at Mount Shasta has me acquainted with this vibration. I vision it is Light sparking all my cells. I feel wonderful, effervescent and alive; a well-tuned humming machine. How lucky to know what actually revitalizes me, this gift of Lord Arcturus and the Arcturian healing masters.

The energy of Arcturus is the energy of Love, the collaborative co-creation made manifest through the mind. Lord Arcturus represents the power of the Heart in pure fluidity with intelligence. He is the point of purity where the Mind of God intersects with the Heart connecting the power of the Heart to the Mind. This connection between Heart and Mind, feminine and masculine, has been disengaged for eons and eons of time. Lord Arcturus is the point re-engaging these connections.

The Arcturians work with all the levels, from the Elohim who are the architects of creation, to Earth's core. Arcturus is one of many entry points and gateways which inter-dimensional beings use to cross the threshold to our planet Earth from other dimensions in our Universe. Sirius and Alpha Centauri are two others. These points of entry serve as energy transformer stations. The atomic structure of Spirit requires a descension of its energy to maintain a physical body on Earth. As we move away from our patriarchal dominant society to the perfect balance of the divine feminine and masculine and open the Heart once again, Lord Arcturus brings the strength and power of God to us through this Arcturian vortex in purity without fragmentation. This is his *Gift Given* to us.

Bathed and refreshed, ready for our next adventure we ask our soul companions to join us and lead the way.

## Shima and Scout—Still Thursday Afternoon Moraine Lake

Many sunlit hours remain in the long summer days of the Northern hemisphere so we head out to Moraine Lake. Compared to this faceted jewel, Lake Louise appears as an unremarkable diamond in the rough. Moraine Lake is smaller than Lake Louise. The mountain peaks spire vertically from the shoreline doubling the impression of their true regal height of over 11,000 feet. It's hard to conceive there could be an even clearer, more translucent, color-perfect turquoise than the waters of Lake Louise, the Canadian Rockies' crown jewel, yet Moraine Lake is.

We're not the only ones with plans to visit this place of majesty. Parking is at a premium and it takes awhile to jostle our way through the crowds. Once again we're struck by the hordes of people in this faraway land. Getting out of the car and walking to the lake a chipmunk spots us and follows along. Too distracted by the human chipmunks, I didn't notice, but Scout, always alert, noticed our follower. We stopped. So did she and looked straight at me. We stared, eye to eye. Scout observed, "She's looking right at you." She's saying, "Shima? Is that you?" I say, "Yes, it's me." And off she goes to alert the other four-legged ones of our arrival.

We take a leisurely walk around the perimeter of Moraine Lake drinking in the nourishment of the waters and reviving our spirits. The water's reflection washes over us, smoothing any rough edges left behind from our day's hike. Clarified, our bodies and souls imbibe the crystal opalescence of Moraine Lake and we are ready to *Journey OM*. Returning to the car, our stomachs are grumbling and our mouths now watering in anticipation of the gourmet cuisine awaiting us back at the Deer Lodge—a place seemingly off the world's culinary map.

It's early and the restaurant is just beginning to stir as we find our table. No matter where we go, it seems Southern California goes too. Seated next to us is a table of three couples, the gilded stereotype of "OC" Orange County. In this sanctuary of natural wonder nestled in the pines and granite peaks, the jewelry is too shiny, the hair too coiffed and the cosmetic procedures too unnatural. We identify what once was.

Yes, I think back on my days running the company Cosmederm and pitching my anti-aging technology. God has taken me on a circuitous route in search of eternal life and beauty; I find reminders of my many selves everywhere I go. Back then I relied on cosmetic procedures, dermatologists, plastic surgeons, and aestheticians to fulfill the face of beauty. Now, I trust that as we enter the higher dimensions we will become ageless, timeless, vibrantly healthy and beautiful through the transformation within.

# MOVING FROM CARBON TO CRYSTALLINE

In early 2009, I completed the physical transformation process of moving from the carbon body to the crystalline body. I share my experience with you, albeit only my experience and devoid of scientific evidence and medical protocol. Nevertheless, it is my truth and my knowing. I understand it is part of my keepership on Earth to be a prototype for this process. There are not many of us on the planet at this time; I am one of the way showers. This process is certainly not the only way, but it is one way to achieve the crystalline Light structure for the new ascended body and can be followed step-by-step with the same results.

Newborns over the last decade come into the world with this blueprint. They are born with this atomic structure and this structure is perhaps the reason young children are so perplexing to the medical profession. Their new crystalline composition could be the cause for their extreme sensitivity to pollutants, chemicals, impure food substances and the like. They're characterized as Indigo children and the Crystal children and more recently (given the rapid acceleration of the ascension process) as the children of the Diamond Ray. There is very little written of these Diamond children and as little as 30,000 are embodied on the surface of Earth. Those of us who were born before this incredible time, when Mother Earth and our physical bodies could not sustain this high Light quotient, must go through a physical transformation while embodied. We all have this blueprint, but it is impossible to resonate with the higher frequencies of the new Earth while still holding the density of the carbon body.

In times past the ability to hold this Light frequency while in physical form was not possible; enlightened souls who reached this frequency ascended from the body. The vibration was simply too high for the density of the carbon body to sustain. In my *at-one-ment* with Chief Joseph I aligned with his highest vibration becoming one with him. This allowed me to merge with his essence and attune to the higher frequencies of the *ascended Chief Joseph* leading me to the emergence of my five higher Light bodies. In my volunteer process for this physical transformation, I opened one of the pathways of ascension for others.

We each have the circuitry—the circulatory and meridian systems—and the mechanics to attune to the higher vibration to which mankind is ascending. The systems are in place. But some individuals aren't conscious of their higher Self so they are not awakened to, or know of, their multidimensional existence. Their life is limited to the restrictions of the third dimension. We are just awakening to the fact that we are multidimensional beings and can live simultaneously on different planes, other dimensions and in parallel realities. It may be overwhelming to our logical mind, but this is the nature of our multidimensional selves and reality—definitely something to ponder.

The stargates I activated on the Chief Joseph trail opened my meridian systems to the cosmic planes. Each time I entered a stargate on the journey I established vibrations and pathways of Light connecting the meridian systems from the Pleiades to the seven stargates. I am conscious now of my omni-dimensionality; my life on Earth influences all the multidimensional selves of my existence and vice versa—as above, so below. The pilgrimage was an opportunity for my soul to synchronize with the intelligence and power of non-physical energies. Physical reality is not solid or static as we might perceive. Physical reality is fluid and ever moving. We must prepare for a new world vision. By its nature the mind is electromagnetic and holographic so when just one individual perceives a peaceful world it makes the way for Peace for All.

The word *ascension* is oftentimes confusing because of its religious connotation. To avoid the bias of the word, you may hear the word expansion used interchangeably with ascension. Expansion's esoteric meaning is limited but it works as a bridge for those who are still dragged down by dogma. What does ascension mean when we are discussing our physical body? Ascension is the atomic structure of the physical body bringing itself into the purity of its origin. When the atom moves back into purity, it becomes pure Light and

Love once again. Ascension is when the critical mass in the physical body is greater Light and Love than the density of separation.

Think of an electron spinning around an atom. The faster the electron spins the greater the space is created. This expanded space allows the cell to hold more light. If there is space for more light the light quotient increases causing the electrons to spin even faster, creating an ever increasing spiral. Light quotient is increased by the electrons spinning faster. When the electrons slow down, velocity decreases and they become dense. In a sense the atom becomes confined. When we focus on purity and clearing the heaviness or density of thoughts or circumstance we free these electrons to spin unencumbered, able to take in more light and align with the higher frequencies of higher resonance. When this happens the electrons spin faster, expansion results and more light can be held in the cell.

We can be *ascended* and still be in physical form allowing a greater opportunity for us to serve mankind. In essence we become *descended masters* able to carry on with our God work in physical form at the highest enlightenment. In past times when a being reached enlightenment the way of ascension was through vacating the physical body. Now with the ability of the body to transform from carbon to crystalline it can hold a much higher Light quotient and still remain in physical form. As one with the whole it is not only humans who are experiencing the ascension process but also Mother Gaia and all of her planetary kingdoms.

Mother Gaia and mankind are undergoing the ascension process together. Like two rock climbers ascending the sheer rock face we have only each other to protect us from the abyss below. Mother

Gaia is the Leader of the climb, responsible for determining the approach, solving problems and placing anchors. Her lead position is not for us. Taking turns we belay for each other feeding out just the right amount of rope to make progress up the climb—never too much. The belay is run through a friction system, a mechanical brake. If we fall the belay system keeps us from plunging to the unfathomed deeps. We ascend back and forth in an ever spiraling ascent beyond our planet, beyond our Milky Way Galaxy to ineffable Universes, all circling into greater Light and Love. As the frequency raises and new energy comes into our planetary body, if we are to remain on Earth, we must align and ascend with the All as divine beings embodied in human form—*divine human beings*. Gift Given; Gift Received.

## FIFTH DIMENSIONAL TELOSIANS

In November 2008, I was guided to take a trip to Mount Shasta. During meditation I was greeted in a vision by Ascended Master Lord Adama the High Priest of Telos. Before our departure I intellectually conceptualized Telos from the books written by Aurelia Louise Jones. This did little to prepare me for the spiritual realization. Telos is a fifth dimensional Lemurian city located a mile deep in the core of Mount Shasta. It has been there since the sinking of Lemuria and safeguards the sacred flames and teachings of that enlightened golden era. The Telosians have just recently begun visiting us on the surface of the planet and are teaching us the ways of fifth dimensional living.

I know this trip was the catalytic event which began the process of transforming my carbon body to crystalline.

I learned from Aurelia Jones that both the Telosian bodies and our human bodies were created with the same divine blueprint. We have the ability to attain the same level of physical perfection as the Telosians. When we open to the knowing that our bodies were created as perfect vehicles and that we were meant to live for thousands of years, we will not show any signs of weakness, aging or dying. As our awareness shifts from the limitations and judgments of the third dimensional consciousness to unconditional Love of the fifth dimension we will raise our bodies' frequency and experience a total rejuvenation and transformation. We will shed our present level of density and become immortal and limitless again. This is the process described as moving from the carbon to the crystalline body.

Many of us have already experienced this phenomenon. We all have the potential to experience this transformation in a relatively short time. Just like the Telosians, our human body will maintain a youthful look between twenty to forty years of age. We can change our looks quite easily at-will and there will be no signs of aging—no wrinkles, no balding, nor will our hair turn grey. Once we dispel the illusion of death we can choose to live for thousands of years without weakness or disease.

## BLESSED HERBS

On the ten-hour drive back from Mount Shasta to San Diego, and still in the consciousness of Telos, I was inspired to internally cleanse my physical body. I chose Blessed Herbs®, a detoxification protocol that systematically cleanses all the bodily systems—the colon, liver and gall bladder, lungs, kidneys and bladder, lymph, blood and skin. This lasted six weeks.

The internal body cleanse was done in precise order. First the colon had to be cleansed so there would be a clear channel for the release of toxins from the other organs. If it were not clear, the excess toxins released from the organs would overtax the elimination system and cause cleansing reactions such as severe and painful headaches, skin eruptions and flu-like symptoms. Elimination is the primary means by which the body gets rids of wastes and toxins. Sweating, exhaling and urinating are others. It is common after years of poor eating, drinking and recreational habits to build up old fecal matter, toxic waste, bacteria and parasites. This plaque on the walls of the intestines lowers the ability to absorb nutrition and creates a toxic environment in our bodies.

The colon, similar to all of our organs and systems retains cellular memory until it can be eliminated from the cells, mucus and fat. Pollution, preservatives, past injuries and long forgotten health problems are all archived in the memory in our cells. During the Blessed Herbs cleanse I discovered in real terms what cellular memory means. As I cleared and released the physical matter of my dietary sins, buried memories from early childhood would surface; unexplained emotion from past experience became present as the mortar of my memories was being chiseled from my cells. I found this fascinating. Emotions of sadness surfaced from my lungs and anger from my liver.

The colon cleanse consisted of a three day pre-cleanse decreasing food portions followed by five days of liquids-only fasting and a sand-like concoction called "Toxin Absorber" mixed with organic unfiltered apple juice. Organic unfiltered apple juice became my best friend! Thankfully, only the colon-cleanse required fasting. The internal cleanse for the other organs relied on a combination of over ninety herbs for their purification process along with eating a vegetarian diet absent of dairy, meat, salt, sugar, white flour and fried foods.

With the colon clean and clear and ready to take on the release of past abuses of the other organs I continued with the liver, gall bladder and para-cleanse...a nice way to say parasites...to me the most awful of thoughts and hard to accept. Unwanted guests! Who me?

If the intestines and colon are not detoxified prior to the liver and gall bladder they will experience a toxic overload, overtaxing their capacity. I am not going to share what I know of unwanted guests. Call it denial of the *ick* factor. Up to 50% of people carry parasites. You can find great sources to learn more if you are called. What I did learn and why it was so important to me to insure I was parasite free is solely spiritual. Parasites are a vehicle for negative entities to attach to the physical body. Once I removed all of the parasites I could no longer be a host to their dense vibrational frequency. There was no magnetic for anything less than the fifth dimension to adhere to. I had just taken a giant step on the ascension ladder.

Coming to Peace with my parasites and bringing the darker aspects of me to the Light I was ready to move on to the lungs, kidneys and bladder. Not nearly as traumatic; I physically moved with relative ease through this stage, however the experience of emotional clearing was pronounced. Makes sense since the kidneys are associated with the emotional element water and the lungs are associated with the emotions of grief, sadness and loss.

Onward to the lymph, blood and skin systems—I was on the home stretch. The lymphatic system and the blood have experienced a flood of toxins as the other organs of the body have released their toxicity during the cleansing. Now it was time to focus on the rivers of life. This stage, too, was uneventful. I recall that I experienced itching in my armpits from the cleansing of the lymph system and as the cleansing moved to the skin I broke out in a rash, nothing noticeable but to my consciousness. Enough already! Even to me, this is too much information!

Finally I was finished. The results were incredulous. My skin glowed. I dropped ten pounds. I felt Light! My mental clarity was keen, even my eyesight improved. I was fully empowered mentally, physically and spiritually. I loved being a spiritual being in a human body. Blessed Herbs. Gift Given; Gift Received.

## THE ION CELL CLEANSE

At the same time I was introduced to the ion cell cleanse. This is a fifth dimensional technology little understood in the third dimension. To the holistic healthcare industry it is described as a foot bath which detoxifies the body, helping to eliminate joint pain and other discomforts. The ionic device sends an electromagnetic pulse through the body. Using different electromagnetic frequencies it increases the speed of the electrons creating more space for Light between the cells. Any lower density element or debris is sloughed off. Documented photo microscopic images of blood cells before the treatment reveal unhealthy, coagulated, malformed cells. After thirty minutes on the machine the cells under the microscope are perfectly spherical. A golden light surrounds each cell—confirmation to me this was working on the Light bodies beyond the physical plane. Twice weekly for a period of three months I used the ion cell-cleanse. The golden light was my affirmation that the ion cell-cleanse possessed miraculous properties.

Scout's experience with the ion cell cleanse was grounded in the physical. In his late teens cruising with friends in the backseat of a '64 Thunderbird, Scout faced a moment he humbly describes as "I couldn't see God but He could see me." One minute careening down the freeway carefree, the next catapulting end over end; the boys' car crashed. Memories still adhere to his reattached finger severed in the accident. As the years passed arthritis set in and surgery and possible amputation of his finger were the recommended treatment. The date for surgery was set for early 2009, six weeks after we had discovered the ion cell cleanse. Scout, who is also playfully called "Skippy the Skeptic" reluctantly joined me in my ion cell cleanse protocol. Within weeks he gained movement in his finger after forty years of immobility. The pain lessened and then ceased. He came to the one and only conclusion…it had to be the ion cell cleanse.

The day approached for the pre-op meeting with the surgeon. Going through the list of preparatory questions, waivers and disclaimers the doctor learned Scout was pain-free and even more amazing could move his finger. Incredulous, the surgeon simply asked, "Then why are you here?" With enthusiasm Scout began to explain until a swift kick by me under the table stopped his oratory, mindful to whom he was speaking. Silence is sometimes the best course.

I have learned to take note of the word *ion* knowing that healing modalities using ionic protocol carry a fifth dimensional frequency. We are all familiar with the feeling of *walking on air* while hiking in the mountains, walking on the beach or stepping under a waterfall. This is where ions are found in abundance; where tens of thousands are created and we feel and experience their full power. In contrast, an average home or office building contains merely hundreds of negative ions, and in many cases, none. There is no doubt that the SETTLEing STONES' effectiveness in reducing stress is partially due to their ionic source.

What is a negative ion? When molecules break apart they are exposed to sunlight, water, wind or radiation which causes them to gain or lose an electrical charge. This creates a negative ion. Negative ions increase the flow of oxygen to the brain. We experience keen alertness, decreased drowsiness and increased mental energy. They also protect us against germs in the air. When negative ions reach the bloodstream they produce biochemical reactions which increase serotonin, helping to relieve stress, alleviate depression and boost daytime energy. The feeling of euphoria we often experience in nature is more than simply being in these wondrous settings. Negative ions can be traced to this euphoric sense of well-being. It is no wonder I spend my life near the ocean and in the mountains sur-rounded by rivers, lakes and waterfalls.

Over the next five months, through a series of energy treatments, Reiki, acupuncture, working one-on-one with spiritual practitioners and undergoing spiritual activations and initiations, I transformed body part by body part, organ by organ, brain, bones, and blood until I was fully embodied as a crystalline structure. I have been advised to be very careful of whom I choose to work on my body. I would most likely baffle traditional medical doctors. Metaphysi-cians and the Arcturian Councils of Light who are master physi-cians and the most highly evolved beings in our Universe, are my most appropriate medical resources.

*The time is NOW. Master Beings have descended to re-matrix our physical fabric, renewing our original blueprint and opening the vortex of Christ Consciousness to bring this higher conscious-ness of who we are into physicality.*

This is my experience through my observation. I am not a scien-tist or a medical professional. There is no scientific or medical accu-racy to my observations. If facts do substantiate what I am about to share, it is not by design. It is my spiritual journey seen through the lens of my soul.

## ENDOCRINE AND LYMPHATIC SYSTEMS

The endocrine system is the electrical switchboard for the human body and the first system required to be recalibrated. Without this circuitry rewired and transformed into the new energy current none of the other organs and systems in my body could be converted into the crystalline structure. Similar to working on any electrical power system, at times I felt shut off during this process and then I would feel a tingling reconnection to my power source upon completion. Of course, just like any electrical system, it must be shut down for repairs! Upon the reconnection I would experience ringing in my ears. Mostly, this took place in my sleep and during dreamtime where I felt extreme, burning heat in my feet. Occasionally I was aware of this process during the day and I literally felt unplugged as things were realigned. Others have reported similar symptoms of not being able to focus clearly.

The lymphatic system in concert with the endocrine system controls the flow of electrical impulses and regulates vibrational frequencies as they move through the body. The lymph nodes act as circuit breakers calibrating the infusion of Light to the level of intensity our consciousness can integrate without causing damage to our bodies. The lymphatic system moves the electrical currents into our cellular structure.

## DNA

My body was renewed into the highest DNA code level I was able to assimilate (which before the stargate pilgrimage was stranded at eighteen). An ascended being in the Adam Kadmon body is stranded at twenty-four DNA. A being who has evolved to twenty-four-strand DNA cannot maintain a physical body—it vibrates too rapidly to hold the density of physicality. A twenty-four strand DNA being is called Adam Kadmon which is the original and perfect blueprint of God's creation of man. In what we call the *fall*, the human being devolved into two strand DNA resulting in the loss of our similitude—Love, Wisdom and Grace—and all of our God-gifted divine human powers. When we talk about moving from Oneness into separation, this was it. Over eons of time we have slowly been evolving back into the perfect blueprint of the Adam Kadmon being God originally created and intended.

## DIGESTIVE SYSTEM

My digestive organs actually took on a new way of working. I could feel it, but I couldn't intellectualize it. I wanted to know more so during a channeling session I asked what happened. I needed to better understand what occurred in my physical body.

*If you were to look at your organs the most appropriate color you would see is opalescence. The reflective capacity of the crystalline structure will now mutate the food you eat into a Light vibration and a Grace vibration. The organs will work with the anatomy of the physical body but they are now working at a code level of DNA that you have accepted. Your medical doctors will not know how to calibrate you so be very careful who you choose to work with you. It will be most appropriate for you to work with your metaphysicians from the Arcturian Councils of Light. The organs have been transformed into their DNA code which is stranded at 18. You will recognize your genius capacity for*

*understanding and will be amazed at what you download and
remember.*

Still seeking greater understanding, during a Lemurian crystal
healing session the practitioner shared her observation with me.
When the crystalline transformation occurred, the digestive organs
began working in a new way; this new way of working was actually
rewritten as a new contract in the Akashic records. I found it interesting in a disbelieving "yeah right" sort of way that something
other than a human being would have an Akashic record. A digestive organ? A contract? Relying on Faith, I accepted that every energetic creation has intelligence, a purpose and contract, and these
contracts are recorded in the Akashic records. Notwithstanding the
suspicion, it was obvious there was a shift in my digestive organs.
My food choices changed. I craved light, easily digestible, water-
dense foods. Small portions satisfied me and digestion was almost
instantaneous. Contrarily, I could also eat anything without reper-
cussion, regardless of how unhealthy or rich—though I am a reverent eater and mindful of my food choices—if I were to indulge—it is
simply transmuted. I lost weight almost effortlessly and regained
my ideal weight from years ago.

Ascension symptoms others have reported during this phase
include common stomach ailments one would usually associate
with digestive disorders, pain in the solar plexus, stomach cramp-
ing, bloating, diarrhea, constipation, food allergies and sensitivity to
gluten, lactose and certain foods, intolerance of preservatives and
processed foods, lack of appetite and lower back pain.

I assumed my next evolutionary step was to *live on Light* and was introduced to the works of Jasmuheen, a beautiful enlightened soul who is showing the way of living on Light. She has over twenty books to her credit and our benefit. Initially, I thought *hers* was *my* path as well, but I learned Jasmuheen's teaching is only one of many ways to transform the human body to a higher crystalline frequency. It is not mine.

I experienced and share another way of transformation. As Chief Joseph so aptly taught me: *All paths are the right path and all lead to One.* I incorrectly surmised that if I were to eat denser, carbon based foods it would lower my Light frequency. Instead I learned that the organs with their new *job description* would mutate the food I ate and therefore the density wouldn't affect the Light frequency I hold. We can also use the breath to transmute food. Hooray! Bring on the ice cream!

But wait. It is important to still eat mindfully with reverence for nature and honor for our body temple. It is still important to remember that fruits and vegetables carry higher frequencies for cellular nutrition than the denser food substances. The word *mutate* is the most precise term I could understand for this process but it is not entirely correct. Perhaps metamorphose. Our *existing* language is languishing behind these fifth dimensional procedures so it is difficult to describe what has no common words. I continue to eat the food I enjoy (some not the best choices), but the genetic imprint of the food as it was originally DNA programmed does not ingrain its imprint into my bodily system. Hmmm…the reflective capacity of the crystalline structure mutates the food I eat into the vibration of Light and Grace.

## THE BRAIN

The next transformation was the brain. Having read that the human brain operates at only 5 percent capacity at our existing stage of evolution, I was excited to discover what this process would reveal in the unexplored 95 percent. When the brain was activated the "race mind" consciousness held in the medulla oblongata was cleared. For a short time, I felt disconnected from society and lacked interest to participate in outside activities. I had little patience for the trifles of the news, the media and other cultural trivia. I now enjoy the daily news and rely on its grounding effects.

Once I released the collective consciousness I opened the way to divine consciousness. The electrical capacity moved very quickly to reformat its synapse and neuro-transmitters and the endorphins increased and flowed unobstructed through my body. I experienced nirvana. Bliss! Before I cleared the path to nirvana, however, an extreme tiredness and heavy headedness came over me. This lasted for a period of two days. This was the expanded energy entering my brain and moving the debris out, debris which was negative thought-forms. Once all of the thought-forms were released, both personal and collective which I had carried lifetime after lifetime through multiple dimensions, my brain stem was organized so as to not allow this mis-qualified energy to return.

I was concerned I would not be able to function in the human world having no point of reference connecting me to mankind. Silly me! This is the enlightenment we are all seeking and yet when it was offered to me I fell into the comfort of my familiar diminished capacity. After all, it was what I was used to. The fear of the unknown tried to stop me, but I volunteered for this pioneering project so I journeyed on. This process was really testing my Faith! Scout's too. Without Faith I would have catapulted into doubt and questioned my sanity. Scout too. I'm relieved that my fears were misguided. I function perfectly well in this world, just not at a third dimension level. This is what the Masters speak of when they say, "*In* the world, but not *of* this world."

As the brain assumes its new support role in the crystalline body some of the symptoms others have shared with me are the feeling of a band of pressure around the forehead and eyes, the inability to concentrate and think clearly, difficulty in focusing on the past or future, directing one's attention only to the present, interrupted sleep and the desire to cocoon in the quiet and dark indoors. There can be a letting go of old relationships and former lifestyle which is all connected to releasing cellular memory. After this laundry list, you must be thinking, "Whoa! Do I really want to venture down this path?" Just know "this too shall pass" and life resumes in glorious splendor. The gifts I received in this process were my increased ability to remember and download information. I gained a greater capacity for understanding. I "just knew" without question. I was rejuvenated and renovated into the harmony of Peace and Light. Gift Given; Gift Received.

Let me mention that this entire process didn't happen all at once and then *voila!* The major transformation occurred over a five month period. I continue to clarify and fine tune. And even though I've reached a level of ascension it does not mean I am bestowed with all the gifts of the Masters. These gifts of clairvoyance, clairaudience, materialization, bi-location and others are realized through practice, not much different than a dedicated athlete preparing for the Olympics.

## THE BONES

The next transmutation was my bones. I imagined my fifth dimensional bones to be super strong like titanium and also extremely porous, flexible and invisible. Light flowed in the place of marrow. Bone marrow is composed of regenerative source energy used by the third dimensional body. My body now uses Light frequency and no longer relies on the biology of the world or the race mind consciousness as source energy. The marrow is transparent and porous allowing these higher frequencies of geometry to move through the skeletal system. My bones are able to accept and hold the energy that is downloaded to me. I am much like a walking Akashic record. This process was like *rattling the cage*, a skeletal *shake-up*. Literally, I was falling head over heels, stepping off curbs and tripping down stairs. It was almost like my physical body was being jolted to momentarily suspend the mental body to allow the new crystalline grids to be integrated in the skeleton. I knew this was all in divine order because I was never injured, but it sure had Scout concerned.

## THE BLOOD

I think of blood as the deepest connecting source of all bodily systems and therefore the most difficult to transcend and transmute. It is the life source of the physical body and the tie that binds us to our ancestral lineage. In the process of transmutation I envisioned an ancient, lifeless tree trunk. I saw Light coming in through my crown chakra, moving into my heart down through my body to the heart of Mother Gaia. The Light was flowing through the trunk and when it reached Earth's inner core and heart of Mother Gaia it began its return path through my body, circling like a figure eight.

On its return the ancient, lifeless tree blossomed into a beautiful vine, full of life force marrow growing and flourishing. When it reached my heart the vine disappeared and morphed into sparklers of formless Light. The blood, now Light elixir, wound its way back to the crown chakra returning to Source. I had contacted the womb of the Mother. My heart became the Heart of the Mother. The life-blood, the connecting cord was showing me the new life. The gift of this transformation is a gift of *no time.* Light, because of its speed, shifts and changes at such a fast vibration I will no longer live through time.

## ARCHANGEL METATRON

Everything was accomplished in a perfect sequence in precise specific order. Archangel Metatron reactivated all of the Light codes in my body. By overseeing the crystalline transformation at every step he protected me from being overwhelmed by my enthusiasm to attain enlightenment. Metatron holds the geometric codes of the original divine blueprint. In the spiritual hierarchy Metatron is the Archangel closest to Source, holding the highest vibration in the formless field of thought-form. He sits at the threshold of the void, where matter is not yet created. His power is to divide the unified

White Light into the spectrum of all colors. This is how he partici-pates in the creation of all things *before* they manifest into matter. Then the archangels and angels take over and manifest this pure thought-form into physical matter. When it is time to return to One-ness Metatron brings form back into the void, the space where everything exists but has not yet been brought into form.

Metatron helps connect us to our own divinity by opening the gates of consciousness. He opens our perceptual abilities so we have the clarity and insight to experience Oneness. He is directly involved with our ascension process helping in every transition, every change and intensification of vibration. On my ascension path Archangel Metatron seemed to be always present at the initiations and activations. Now I understand why. He has been my teacher along with Lord Sananda in understanding the role of a *descended master*, still in the body united with the Holy Spirit. I found working with Metatron challenges me to connect with rarified vibrations and frequencies I have not experienced. I have learned to call on him with great respect and mindfulness, for he is more than willing to accommodate my requests for ascension, oftentimes at my own physical peril. Like an insatiable child near the untended cookie jar, I cannot get enough of the Love and Light that he is ready to bestow, and like the child with too much of a good thing, I find myself out of body.

The endocrine system was recalibrated to hold the perfect Adam Kadmon, the divine human man in the image of God. Then the bone marrow and the skeletal system were upgraded to support this new Light sustaining it. The brain was activated, opening it for high frequency downloads and the blood system was cleansed of ancestral lineage now flowing pure elixir of Light. The order was very specific and for very specific reasons. At every restructure there was the possibility of failure. Had the Masters working with me not been careful I could have been moved out of the body. My spirit would not have been able to withstand the crash of imbalances. This reformation of the body is as new to the Masters working on this physical transformation as it is to us. I am a prototype and have been told there are 1,100 other people on Earth undergoing the same transformation simultaneously. I can't wait to meet them and share notes! My volunteer service is showing the Ascended Masters how to gently and successfully bring the geometries of Light and Love into the physical body. We are soul companions working together for the benefit of All. Our promise to our brothers and sisters is that no one will be left behind. We all will return to Source, Father/Mother God. There is no other way. We are all One.

Each of the neurons in my physical body and the neuro-receptors of my emotional body were energized with a new electromagnetic vibration. My bio-spiritual body was altered and transcended. Through spiritual initiations and Light activations my DNA strands have slowly increased from 2 to 12 to 18 and after the Chief Joseph pilgrimage I hold 21 strand DNA. In *Journey OM, A Soul Journeyer's Adventure* I describe in detail the spiritual concept of DNA and its role in our enlightenment. Eventually there will be a total synthesis of all dimensions. At this time I am reaching the 9th dimension. The Mahatma is a great teacher and mentor whom I call on to help me understand. This transformation of my physical body is perfectly aligned with the other three lower bodies—etheric, mental and emotional. Once my four lower bodies merged in perfect alignment I could fully integrate my "I AM" Presence into my physical body and begin the activation of the five higher Light bodies—Electromagnetic, Epi-kinetic, Eka, Gematrian and Zohar.

The next gift will be enhancing physical beauty. This excites me—ageless, timeless beauty! As I bring in more Light, healing will be spontaneous and I will begin to see very little aging. I will be able to enhance my physical beauty in any way I choose. Babaji will mentor me on creating the ageless/timeless physical form. He will teach me the skills of materialization, dematerialization, bi-location, teleportation and the other gifts of mastery to freely navigate multidimensions. I wait patiently. Patiently I wait. If I choose, this will be the body I ascend with, to use eternally whenever I visit this lovely blue-green planet Earth. Or I can choose to put on a different *garment* to suit the visit. Free will!

My pathway to enlightenment didn't have a lot of direction and guideposts. At the time there wasn't much written about the ascension process and its symptoms; I relied on Faith and Trust. God left me a few clues here and there but I was basically left alone. There weren't a lot of tangibles to tether to. So I created my own small rituals which always brought God top of mind. Mindfulness in everything I do and engaging all of my senses was the fast track for me to enlightenment…and continues to be.

At first I dedicated a special time and space for meditation. I had my altar, my candles, my incense and my special cushion only for this purpose. Religiously I would awaken in the early dawn hours to connect to my higher Self. Eventually consciousness was no longer confined to this cage I'd created and became part of every waking moment. I still love to meditate for the simple joy of silence, but not for the reasons before.

I chose each day's awakening and the everyday task of bathing and showering to create my mindful moments of spirituality. Something I could rely on happening each and every day. Each morning I awaken and break our nighttime fast with fresh squeezed citrus before Scout and I walk the hills and trails of San Dieguito Park bordering Lake Hodges. Sometimes we walk for exercise, most often just to be in the presence of the hawks, the ravens, the waterfowl, loons and heron; rabbits and gophers. I pace my steps to the rhythm of my mala.

Returning home I light incense and choose my favorite music, Carlos Nakai's flute, Deva Primal, Snatam Kaur or Chloe Goodchild. Then I draw a bath infused with Epsom salt and Celtic sea salt to help regulate the electric impulses being re-circuited through my body in the integration process. The added benefit of Epsom salt is magnesium's soothing and mood-elevating properties. Occasionally I will switch it up and add baking soda if I feel a detoxification is necessary.

Early on my spiritual path I was introduced to Amrita Essential Oils, the most rarified and pure essential oils I could find. Essential oils are the concentrated intelligence of the plant kingdom. Their etheric influence is the connection to the mind and body through the nervous system. They are the integrating force for the healing intelligence and require respect and knowledge in their use. The flower essence reaches the deepest core of our being stimulating inner transformation. I purchase unscented lotion or almond oil and each morning according to my mood I select a few drops of essential oil and mix with the lotion. Some mornings it's *Evergreen Heaven* if I'm craving the pine scented mountain air, or *Citrus Bliss* if I'm feeling playful, or *Spiritually Awakening* and the scent of sandalwood if I am especially reverent. Over time the pure fragrance of flowers and herbs became more alluring than perfume.

You may be ready to stop reading right here thinking, "Yeah, right, sounds good, but who has time for this? I've got kids to awaken and dress and lunches to make, all before getting to work on time!" My morning practice begins at 7:30 a.m. and I am dressed and ready for my day by 9:00 a.m. My daily practice takes much less time than sharing it with you. And it did not all converge at once. I discovered these gifts and developed this beautiful lifestyle a little at a time. If it seems beyond the bounds of possibility perhaps consider a special day for your practice or adding a single note to your daily song. I live a rich life—not expensive—enriched.

I finish with a practice I started years ago, balancing my chakras with special chakra oil blends from a Canadian company, Colour Energy®. In my ascension process when the chakras merged from singularity into a column of Light it became unnecessary for me to delineate each chakra and bring it into balance. The ritual is beautiful and something Scout and I share together so I continue the practice. There is a special chakra oil blend for each chakra. Together we place a few drops of each of the oils on our chakras. With a quick kiss this ends our morning and we're off to dress and depart.

Throughout this entire process I was in the Hand of God through the Ascended Masters and my human colleagues. From my experience and with the assurance and assistance of my teachers Lord Melchizedek, Babaji, Metatron and the Mahatma, I am confident about sharing and teaching this process of transmutation and transformation to you. I eagerly offer my assistance so you may gracefully evolve into the crystalline structure without fear of harm. If this is your calling, your simple conscious intention and desire will accelerate your process. Like me, you may not be conscious of this transformation. Faith and Trust and your willingness to be the greatest expression of God's Love are the key. Trust is the key uniting self and Divine Self. It is the ultimate moment when the soul chooses a physical experience and gives itself to physical manifestation and becomes flesh. Trust is a knowing that the human physical body carries the knowledge of its God Source and will never be separate from the One. Always Trust that all is for the highest good and in perfect divine order and allow any discomforts to serve as guideposts.

Allow. Bring in the energy of Peace and ascension and the Office of Christ to assist you and keep it flowing. Bless the water you drink and immerse in its healing properties. Eliminate table salt. It has a chemical misconstruction that affects the waterways of the body and purposely lowers the vibration. Find Light workers and spiritual healers who are enlightened to the carbon to crystalline body transformation. Join them in this journey of self discovery. Be the gift to one another to show the way. This was truly my beginning of living as a descended master on Earth, stepping into my God Presence as an avatar of Peace. I was ready to answer my God calling and step into my garment of Light.

# SHIMA AND SCOUT
# STILL DINNER—THURSDAY
# DEER LODGE RESTAURANT

Dinner. Yes, we're still at the table. It was only a glance at our "OC" gilded diners that sparked this cellular memory. What took pages to share was only an instantaneous reflection of a soul extension of Darcy as the Cosmederm executive relying on cosmetic procedures to face the world. I smile as I realize how the past became present by simply bringing the memory into the now. I begin to understand the teachings of Eckhart Tolle. His precepts aren't as difficult as I was making them: Living in the moment—staying in the now—being present. Simplicity is sometimes difficult to grasp.

We direct our attention to the menu. It mirrors our locale and we are entertained by the entrées of Rocky Mountain game platter, grilled buffalo ravioli, ranch elk sirloin and wild caribou medallions—each item an entrée to the wild animal kingdom. We choose the plant kingdom and share asparagus leek and potato chowder with red pepper oil, a salad of grilled asparagus and artichoke, baby heirloom lettuce, vine-ripened tomatoes with sherry, grape seed oil vinaigrette. I choose the butternut squash ravioli, fennel, arugula, hazelnut butter and manchego. Scout never resists what he rarely cooks at home. For his entrée he selects roast lamb rack, pumpkin-seed pesto crust, asiago potato mash and grainy mustard jus. Ah, mountain air, exercise and food to delight the senses and nourish the cells. We've discovered *soul food* and our bodies love us!

It is past 9:00 p.m. and the sun has yet to crest the mountain peaks as we head across the road for an after dinner walk. We follow a path winding along Louise Creek. It's late in the season and yet the waters flow with abundance. No sign of lack. The creek banks are lined with a potpourri of color. Scout gathers an evening bouquet for me of heart leafed arnica, cow parsnip, scarlet paintbrush, poppies and fireweed. God is smiling! *Journey OM.*

# SHIMA AND SCOUT
# THE RING OF LIGHT

*There will be a ring of Light that you will see. Watch for the ring of Light. You will know the signs. It may be a ring around the moon, a ring around the sun, maybe a radiant ring coming like a rainbow. It may be a ring of water that spreads from the center of a stone dropped in the lake. There will be a radiant ring. This is the sign when all of the ancestors will begin to pray with you. All of the spirits will pray for the flowing of this great abundance, this ascension way.*

Words heard weeks ago. I was excited when I received this clue to the treasure hunt. With no immediate revelation I archived it in the vault of my mind, submerged, but with the energy imprinted for a simple *Aha* moment when the prophecy would be revealed. And sure enough, that revelatory moment when the radiant ring came in sight occurred early evening on August 6th at Moraine Lake.

While walking the shoreline of the lake, Scout and I were intrigued by bubbles gurgling to the surface from the lakebed. They glimmered in the sunlight carrying bursts of light in each sphere. So unusual and beautiful was this sight we stopped to ponder. Were these little microscopic animals? Was it geothermal activity? We watched, our interest keyed and curiosity piqued. With no clear explanation we continued on.

Later, settling in for the night, like mother to child—Shima to Scout—I read the message from Chief Joseph in preparation for the next day. When we got to the part: *There will be a ring of light that you will see...*we stopped smiled and burst into awareness. The bubbles! Rings of Radiant Light!

**The Harp Angel at the Fairmont Chateau**

The Teahouse atop Plain of Six Glaciers

*Ho Va ah aunm*
*Into the Womb*
*Ho Va ah aunm*
*Humni Mother's birth*
*Ascension on Earth*
*Back to the One*
*Where we've begun*
*Ho Va ah aunm*
*Children Come Home*

**Elevation Gain**: 370 m (1215 ft)
**Maximum Elevation**: 2100 m (6890 ft)
**Trailhead**: The northeast corner of Lake Louise pass in front of the Chateau Lake Louise after crossing from the large public parking areas using either of two footbridges over Louise Creek.

**0.0** – Sign at junction (elevation 1730 m). Stay on left along the north shore of Lake Louise, as for the Lake Louise Lakeshore trail.
**2.1** – End of the Lake Louise Lakeshore trail at a rest bench (1740 m) above the west end of Lake Louise. Descend a short distance to travel beside the braided channels of Louise Creek.
**2.5** – Begin gradual climb at two rest benches where Louise Creek is a single stream funneled through rocky banks.
**3.4** – Junction (1800 m) with bottom of Shortcut Switchbacks to Plain of Six Glaciers trail from the Highline trail. Keep straight.
**4.1** – Junction with the Highline trail for Lake Agnes. Keep left. The trail stays fairly level for some distance and passes along a narrow ledge (there is an alternative route along the base of the cliff). Then begin a steady climb in the trough behind the north lateral moraine of the Lower Victoria Glacier.
**5.2** – Series of four short switchbacks.
**5.5** – Plain of Six Glaciers teahouse (2100 m).

**Passage from my journal—A song begins**

Plain of Six Glaciers Tea House
Salon de thé Plaine des Six Glaciers
100 m
Plain of Six Glaciers Lookout
Plaine des Six Glaciers
1.4 km
Washrooms
Toilettes
Horse Trail
Sentier équestre

Mount Shasta, November 2008

Blessed Herbs, Thanksgiving 2008

Passage from my journal—Gathering flowers along Louise Creek

Heart Leefed Arnica
Cow Parsnip

An "ah ha" moment the evening of August 7th. At Moraine Lake we were intrigued by bubbles coming up from the bed of the lake. Was it little animals? Was it geothermal activity. We watched but without knowing. Later while getting ready for bed I read the transmission from Chief Joseph aloud to Jim. When we got to the ring of light — Jim said, "that was the bubbles." Oh Thank you, God, for Jim.

**Passage from my journal—Moraine Lake**

Early morning on Moraine Lake

# FRIDAY, AUGUST 7

## SHIMA AND SCOUT

Yesterday morning when we awoke the air hung heavy. As the sun tried to break through it reflected the mist casting a glowing mirage. Light was emanating upward in perfect geometric patterns. It was then I knew—that would be the spot. Lake Louise is an enormous vortex of Mother Goddess. It is a trinity gate, the place where a mountain portal, a water portal and the internal Earth's molten rock core converge; a center point of synergy creating electromagnetic force fields around Earth and the spheres beyond gravity. Deep, deep into the water there is an obelisk, an enormous stone, shaped like the mountain's sharp peak, a pyramid. The obelisk is symbolic of the connection with God Source. It is part of the trinity gate assisting Mother Gaia to receive Light and Love and hold the energy in its absolute form to co-conceive with it. The trinity gate will assist the stargate in staying open.

Today would be a practice run. There was no time for error. The sun would strike the water's surface in an exact moment, a split second and the touchdown would be complete. We must time our wake-up, pack up and cast off to meet future on *her* terms. Tomorrow would be the real deal, opening the eighth stargate, the *Ascension Gate.*

## STARGATES, PORTALS, VORTEXES, AND GRIDS

I recall it was only four short months ago when I was asked by Chief Joseph to open stargates and fulfill his destiny. Back then I did not even know what a stargate was. I had heard of portals, vortexes and grids and I tossed the words about carelessly in conversation without understanding. Yes, I had been to Sedona and other known vortexes. I had even created *Elohim Peace Waters*, a Peace Waters product from the Elohim Peace *portal* in Whitefish. But if asked, "What is a portal?" I could only mumble an answer hopefully disguising my half-knowing in a jumble of confusion. Part of the reason this topic of stargates, vortexes, portals and grids is so difficult to grasp is that it deals with dimensions and planes which exist beyond our third dimension. Now I am ready to truly understand the meaning of these intricate, complex connections to the cosmos.

## FOLLOW TO THE POINT OF KNOWING

In *Journey OM, A Soul Journeyer's Adventure*, I describe stargates as "an etheric inter-dimensional energy alignment between two points in interstellar space," a definition I found on the internet. How confusing is that? Even now, as I rewrite these words I am not clear. I hide my ignorance in complex words strung together in compound sentences. Now I will explain these inter-dimensional connections from the Wisdom of my Heart. This seemingly simple exercise is profound for me. It is my initiation from student to teacher. What is important to remember about sharing my/our experience with God is that our experience captures our being in a moment of time. What I perceive to understand of this vast Universe is my Truth *only* in this moment, *only* at this level of my being.

We are forever spiraling and ever expanding to greater awakening and awareness of the wholeness of the Universe. We build on Truth, more pieces of the puzzle come into play and our knowledge expands. I look back on my *Aha* moments, those revelations of all-knowing and ponder, "How could I think that, when now I know this?" We are all on our spiritual path to Oneness. Our paths criss-cross and each *Aha* is a signpost for others to follow. Some choose the gentle path leading through the meadow while the extreme journeyer may scale the cliff side. It's our choice which path to follow, or do we wish to blaze a new trail of our very own? This writing reflects my knowing at a point describing time. Truth holds eternal but at a different point in future time a shortcut may be discovered and the path I trek now may be overgrown when you come upon its signposts.

Ohiyesa, an esteemed member of the Sioux Dakota nation walked his spiritual path at the time of Chief Joseph. He was the bearer of Universal Wisdom and the bridge to the higher spiritual vision of mankind. He worked for America to become "One with an honest and indigenous soul." He was guided by his grandmother's sage Wisdom: *When you see a new trail, or a footprint you do not know, follow it to the point of knowing.* Her words are meant for me, too. The footprints of the many Masters before me have guided me to this point of knowing. May you pick up from here and *Journey OM.*

## ROCKS, STONES, AND WISDOM

I turn to my teachers, the rocks, stones, and crystals, to help me understand the pathways and Light streams of our Universe. Crystals and stones have held mystical meanings and revealed the mysteries of the Universe before the dawn of our short history. Native American holy men, ancient Gypsy seers, Oracles of Delphi and Aboriginal hunters all have worn stones as talismans, used crystals and stones in their healing practices and relied on crystals for divination. Stones have a spirit or energy within that can be called upon for aid, support and insight. Rocks, stones, and crystals, carry the pure frequency of Universal sound vibrating at a lower density. Energy of the cosmos is powerful beyond comprehension; our current energy field cannot integrate this pulse into useable form. We would simply *short out.* The mineral kingdom holds a stepped down version of these cosmic frequencies of Light and Love in a form whereby we can safely access the higher dimensions while being in our physical bodies.

## CRYSTAL HEALING NAPS

I prepare for a *crystal nap* where I lay down and strategically place chosen crystals and stones along meridian lines and chakras. I set my intention to understand the stargates and portals, light-ways and byways that link our planet to the Universe. The practice of the laying on of stones is ancient. The stones and crystals act as transmitters or receivers. By tuning into their vibration I can adjust my vibratory frequency to resonate with theirs and tap into the field of Wisdom I wish to explore. Crystals and stones are conscious beings; however, unlike humans they have never experienced separation, form and formless, matter and Spirit are One. They are the pure record keepers of Source Wisdom.

I choose galactic stones from my rock collection and ask for the galactic emissaries to enlighten me with the knowledge of stargates, portals, vortexes and grids. First, I place the Illuminite from the sacred Crystal Hill in the Mojave Desert on my solar plexus. Light Beings of the galactic plane use Illuminite as a beacon—similar to a lighthouse—signaling to seekers who attune to its resonance through the veils of the Earth plane. Illuminite is a protector from lower frequencies and helps raise one's vibration to the fifth dimensional frequency of Peace, Love and Harmony.

Next I place Azeztulite between the solar plexus and heart chakra. Azeztulite has an amazing birth story found in Robert Simmons work entitled, *The Book of Stones.* This is quartz discovered in North Carolina and Vermont. It takes its name from the light beings the Azez who infuse this simple stone with their galactic frequency. Azeztulite assists in inter-dimensional travel and exploring alternate realities.

On my throat chakra I place a small piece of Covellite which is mined alongside copper in the Butte, Montana mines. Covellite increases psychic abilities and inner vision bridging the higher and lower worlds and opening the channel for divine communication.

In the palm of each hand I hold a Pleiadian Love stone connecting to the feminine Christ Consciousness. Pleiadian Love stones are rare, smooth and rounded, ocean-tumbled quartz. Found only between winter solstice and spring equinox along the Southern California shoreline, they carry the divine feminine energy of the Pleiades and Mother Earth infused with the fifth dimensional frequencies of unconditional Love.

Lastly, I place Moldavite on my 3$^{rd}$ eye. Moldavite is a star-born stone crashed from a meteor in the area of the Czech Republic approximately 14.8 million years ago. It is the stone that awakened me to remembering my Pleiadian star seed lineage and gifted me with my God work. So pivotal is Moldavite to the spiritual awakening of mine and others' souls that I will share my story. It may be your wake-up call too!

## MOLDAVITE

My fascination for rocks and crystals goes back to the age of seven, but never in my years as a rock hound had I seen Moldavite—until two years ago while browsing in a bookstore. I like to play a game where I select a book and whatever page it randomly opens to is the message meant for me. This day I picked up a book on crystals and gems, and playing along, it opened to Moldavite. Interesting, nothing more. I was impressed by its ancient age and origin, some hypothesize Pleiades, but I quickly forgot about it. The following day I stopped by a bead store to have a necklace repaired. While paying for the service I looked down into the display case and saw a pendant. Having just seen the picture of this dark, emerald-green glass look-alike I inquired, "Is that Moldavite?" "Yes," the sales associate replied with an eerie reverence in her voice. I looked at it through the glass but did not touch it, resistant to the price. However, a prompting nudged me into asking if there were any loose stones perhaps not quite as expensive. I followed the woman to another cabinet and a small tear drop piece immediately grabbed me. I picked it up and a jolt of energy from my crown chakra to the tips of my toes surged through me. I couldn't release the stone from my palm. This was mine. I knew I had to have it—at any cost. Synchronicity was in play and Moldavite was leading the way.

Nothing is random. Everything emerges from Divine Plan. The Universe works in perfect divine order. The relevance in sharing the following sequence of my enlightenment is to illustrate how seemingly isolated encounters over irrelative time spans can come together in a singular moment illuminating the entirety of one's soul's journey. Like the childhood game *Dot to Dot* I connected words and chance meetings to picture my destiny. What do your *dots* reveal?

**Spring 2005**—I met with a potential business client named **Catherine**. We added each other to our e-mail lists, nothing more.

**Summer 2006**—More than a year later I meet with a channel who foretells of the importance of my past life in the 1800s as a **Native American UTE** medicine woman. So? I can't figure it out and I file it away.

**September 1, 2007**—Two years later after first meeting **Catherine**, I receive an email from **Catherine** who was guided by her Higher Self to invite me to a gathering with **Judith K. Moore.** In Judith's biography she describes receiving a sacred bundle from **Native American UTE** elders. **UTE** gets my attention. Everything is in place and speeding up.

**September 13, 2007**—I open a book and chance on **Moldavite**, a stone possibly from **Pleiades**, and didn't think twice about it.

**September 14, 2007**—I see **Moldavite** for the first time while running an errand and think twice, making an impulse buy!

**September 15, 2007**—I attend the seminar with **Catherine** and **Judith K. Moore**. It rouses my memory that I carry the codes of the **Pleiadian** Christ Consciousness and the **Native American** soul lineage connecting me to **Chief Joseph**. Goose bumps. The story goes on.

**September 18, 2007**—Three days later I am laid-off, unemployed.

**Catherine—Judith—UTE—Moldavite—Pleiades—Native American—Chief Joseph—Here I AM!**

In what seemed like an instant I was ejected from my career identity and propelled into my God work as a soul journeyer fulfilling unfinished destinies, as an avatar of Peace. For years unbeknownst I had been guided down a specific path to this moment in time at

Lake Louise where I will open the eighth stargate, the *Ascension Gate*. Little did I know, *dot to dot* the picture comes into view of Shima, *I AM* that *I AM* my shining God Presence.

## STILL CRYSTAL NAPPING

Oh yes, back to the crystal nap where I am intent on seeking the knowledge of stargates, portals, vortexes and grids. I understand this tome without time may be difficult for you to follow if you are reading linearly. I empathize with your thinking, "Where is she taking me now?" Every now and again I ask, "How can I fathom sharing my multidimensional musings held together by the invisible threads of my knowing? Do I have the courage to share a memoir more cosmic than human? And why? And then I am reminded from Source that I am simply under contract and if it is Thy Will, who am I to question content? My Higher Self steps in, my ego steps out, and I Trust. *Just do it. Journey OM.*

Like *Journey OM, A Soul Journeyer's Adventure* the genuine value of this book is the interactive Light and Love it transmits. It is written on two levels requiring passage from the Earth grids into the Spiritual grids. The Ascended Masters are the writers of these spiritual lessons, Universal Truth and Wisdom. I am the author. My contribution is to keep you interested and your ego occupied in order that you can receive the embedded Light codes.

With stones in place, I lay still, invoking the Wisdom of the Mineral Masters. I am gone for less than an hour. It feels like nothing more than a nap, but the awakening is like returning from the abyss. I have been taken from the body to an ashram of learning and then returned. I have no bearings—where am I—what time is it? I've awakened ahead of my body. Or has my body awakened ahead of me? Once back down to Earth and fully integrated, I share stargates, portals, vortexes and grids.

To fathom this cosmic freeway requires us to expand our consciousness to the realization of the Universe as a whole, all working together in a universal system. These are pathways from the highest level of Source spiraling through all dimensions to the tiniest particle of life in the first dimension. These pathways are how Source energy radiates through Creation. They create pathways for the highest levels of energy to be stepped down from universal, galactic, solar and planetary levels into all dimensions. Portals, vortexes and stargates number in the billions; they function with precise mathematical accuracy.

We discovered just how exact their location while traveling along Chief Joseph's Trail. Using the pendulum, if we were even a few feet away from the stargate we would render a negative reading. Once we determined the exact spot the pendulum would swing *Yes* wildly. It amazed us that the location was so precise in an expanse of land hundreds of miles wide. It took my logical mind quite some time to forego the idea that *anywhere in the area would do just fine.*

Everything down to the smallest subatomic particle works together in great harmony with ease and efficiency. If things did not operate with such mathematical accuracy tremendous chaos would occur.

We also learned that each stargate had a gatekeeper and until we identified the gatekeeper—a rock outcropping, an unusual land formation, or a variant plant species—we could not enter. There is an evolved being, usually from the angelic kingdom, the devic realm or extraterrestrials resonating with the level of frequency for each particular vortex, portal and stargate guarding these sacred openings. No one can travel freely through portals or gateways to dimensions higher than their level of consciousness. Unless resonance is matched, entry may be denied in order to safeguard the purity and efficiency of these sacred sites. The guardians prevent unwanted energies from infiltrating these sites of absolute purity and Wisdom.

Permission to enter is sometimes granted to souls who are not at that vibrational level if an Ascended Master agrees to sponsor and accompany them. Through invocation and gratitude we were allowed entrance to these sacred openings on our pilgrimage. Most often we were not conscious of our travel which occurs in the twinkle of an eye. The specific stargates along the Chief Joseph path are the energy alignment connecting the constellation Pleiades to stargates on Earth. They are a living pathway of Light from Earth to Pleiades. These stargates were anchored by Chief Joseph in 1877 and activated—hard to believe—by me!

There are many types of and uses for portals, stargates and vortexes. Some are used for stepping down vibration so we can assimilate higher frequencies in a useable form. Spacecraft use these dimensional freeways for travel. They are used to teleport between dimensions, planets, solar systems, galaxies and Universes. On our stargate journey we reopened a portal at Tolo Lake. It is a time in Nez Perce history I like retelling…one of community, joy and Peace before white man's illusion darkened God's vision of Love.

Tolo Lake's history is frozen in the ice age, a place where wooly mammoths roamed. More recently, in 1877, it was the place called Tepehlewam by the Nez Perce—a sacred site where friends and relatives of other tribal bands would gather to prepare their winter food supply. It was a time of yearly celebration. The old men gambled the time away, the young braves raced their horses in hopes of catching the eye of young maidens; the women dug camas bulbs sharing stories with their sisters since the last year's harvest. All was not celebration this year of 1877, however. While the camas gathering, racing, gambling, flirting and playing were going on the chiefs and elders were deep in counsel facing the difficult choice of moving to the reservation or not.

In 2009, we were drawn to this place. It held Chief Joseph's vision of *One People and Earth as our Mother* (before she was considered a commodity by the Americans to be bought and sold). *We are all alike—brothers of one father and one mother—with one sky above us and one country around us and one government for us all. And all people are one people.*

Tolo Lake is on the planetary meridian system, an energy line for the planetary migration route. It is an inter-dimensional meeting point connecting Earth to all dimensions. In ancient times, highly evolved spiritual beings would teleport to Tolo Lake from the portal sites of Stonehenge, the Himalayas, Mount Shasta, Machu Pichu and others. For some reason, Tolo Lake had shut down. Reopening it was part of our God work on the Chief Joseph stargate pilgrimage. Scout playfully renamed it *Tolo Portal*. From then on, when it was time to *Journey OM*, Scout would shout: *"And now we Tolo Portal!"* This short, benign behest carries the key to inter-dimensional travel. You can use it in your inter-dimensional travel.

# SHIMA AND SCOUT
# SUNRISE PRACTICE RUN

We're aroused by the buzzing wake up call and reluctantly crawl out of our warm bed. Why are we doing this? After all, it's just a practice run. The first steps, feet hitting floor, remind us of our long hike yesterday. Warming out of our stiffness we dress and depart. Thinking we will be the only ones out at sunrise we are surprised by others with the same intention to experience Mother Gaia's good morning call. The night has not yet bid adieu and the full moon is a draw to those who dare the damp and cold. Scout quotes Mother Moon as she sinks behind the glacier, "I now present you Father Sun."

It is crowded. Scout doesn't want to walk further. "We'll miss the moment," he says. I insist. Meditation is out of the question here among the hordes. The human chipmunks are eager for the day to begin. No silent, slow start for them. I remember my annoyance from yesterday and I let it go. It is what it is. No sense denying it. Like pulling a wagon with a bent wheel I bring Scout along until we find the perfect spot along the shoreline, away from the early morning risers. Yet even the occasional canoer is chipper breaking the morning solace and the constant whir of generators from the City of Chateau mars the silent beauty.

I make space in my irritation. Now we wait for the sun to rise, for the pristine moment when fire meets water. It happens. The sun strikes. It is blinding in its splendor. I think, "This is what God wants. See Him. See His Creation and be in joy." This is practice for tomorrow's event and yet I think ascension has always been. We are the ones who are awakening to our ascension. It has always been here. It is not an event coming to Earth. We are the ones grasping the Hand of God reaching for us. I bathe in the light of His Love. This is a practice run. Or so I think. Tomorrow will bring the real thing; tomorrow will be when the first rays of the radiant ring kiss open the *Ascension Gate.*

I try to write, but it takes my eyes from Sun's glory. I try to look, but it is too brilliant for my human eyes. I try to imagine what life was like before this moment. Like the wedding rehearsal we prepare, but nothing will match the moment when God says, "Enough of these veils, nothing can stand between My Love for you. I will hold back no longer."

## SCENT OF THE PINE

This is too much radiance for my ego. My mind starts wandering and my ego jumps in. "Oh yea," it says, "at last a way back." The ego is uncomfortable in its new role of supporter and tempts me into remembering my fitful dreams last night, pressuring me to sort them out. I don't understand how, if we have awakened to ascension, dreams can be any less than Peace, Love and Harmony? And yet, I dream of unsettling scenarios. Where do these dreams arise? Are they remnants of past memories, cleared from the physical body and now dwelling in the astral realms? Are they mine to rectify from other lifetimes, or have I tapped into the archives of collective consciousness and it is my service to free these enduring thought-forms?

I am blind to these dreams' higher purpose and do not give them their rightful due nor thanks for their invisible message. Blessed we are, to be able to transmute much of our karma through dreamtime, eliminating the requirement to release past karma in real life situations with the real possibility of creating new karma in the process. There is a way to abdicate our third dimension dreams. Before we sleep we can ask the Ascended Masters to take us to one of the ashrams of higher learning where dreams are at bay and we spend our dreamtime in our God Presence, in joy and training with our soul companions. We simply need to ask. This is the *Gift Given*.

This time, when the ego tempts me into the unreal world of worry and fear, something different occurs. I am diverted…by the scent of pine. The forest balm lures me from the ego's clutch, drawing my attention. I return from this troublesome *daydreaming* by the overpowering scent of pine. I wake up to nature's aroma and am brought back from this train of thought to the present moment where fitful dreams don't exist.

I stop. I inhale. In my excitement of this sensual discovery I interrupt Scout from his thoughts to breathe with me the intoxicating mixture created by pine and pitch. I sense where my ego was taking me and am conscious of the moment when my God Presence intervened with the scent of nature's forest. In the moment I choose God and say, "No thank you, ego. I don't need to go there. Not interested in your story." The ego foiled again! And I smile. I am beginning to *sense* my way through the maze of the third dimension and remain in the higher realms. The scent of the trail—another gift and tool received on this journey. The ego is muted…for now. Gift Given; Gift Received.

My challenge on this pilgrimage has been to find Peace with the people, to be *in* this world and not *of* this world, focused and centered, unaffected by what surrounds me. It has been an unrelenting lesson. It is at every turn. Yesterday while talking myself into *being in Peace* (which wasn't working by the way), I was again taken in by the scent of pine. Enraptured, it left me no choice but to dwell on only it. My petty chatter was silenced and I forgot my irritation. In that split second I was gifted the tool of transformation and transmutation. At any moment in any situation the scent of pine invites me into a state of Grace showing me the way to Peace. Back home when I return from this pine-scented wilderness I have the essential oil blend *Evergreen Heaven.* I will use it with new reverence and use it wisely.

## PEACE TO THE POWER LINES

The constant parade of people is not the only distraction. The roar of hotel generators is only silenced by the river's thundering, pouring over the glacier boulders, drowning each other in competition. It's a recurring theme, this duality of noise pollution. Why duality? We merged duality at *Swallows Window* and *Heart of the Golden Rose* so I don't understand why all is not in Harmony; why sound reverberates as noise not music. Then I remember *Peace to the power lines.*

One afternoon my friend Velvet and I took off hiking in the Columbia Range near Glacier Park in search of a rose quartz vein from the abandoned Tea Kettle mine. Chances were slim we would find such a treasure, but like Hansel and Gretel we love to create excursions for our spiritual play. Rose Quartz is one of the most important stones of our time. Its gentle, tender energy integrates Love and Compassion, opening the heart chakra and expanding our capacity to give and receive Love. The soothing vibration of Rose Quartz carries the energy of the divine feminine and resonates with Archangel Chamuel. Its energy releases tension, stress, anger and resentment. Rose Quartz is energizing to the heart and focuses on internal self-love. The gentle, loving Rose Quartz opens us to our divine purpose showing the way of unconditional Love.

Aligned with the energy of Rose Quartz we followed an old logging road. As we climbed the face of the mountain we crossed under huge electrical transformer towers. The Earth vibrated and the air hummed with the electrical energy pulsing through its wires. Not far from these towering lines was the Hungry Horse Dam whose waters birthed their electrifying power. This disruption of nature drove us to anger. All the negative things we had been told about power lines began to surface: the incidence of breast cancer among men who give their lives to the power lines, the studies of harmful effects from living near transmission sites and the undeniable ugliness of their imposing structures.

Our judgment and the judgment of our communities were unleashed. And then a feeling of sadness washed over us. The Love of Rose Quartz was working its miracle. What we perceived to be the desecration of this pristine forest marred by these steel giants and their unearthly screech was birthed from what we Love—the Water. We saw, perhaps for the first time, the source of this energy we were cursing was the Water we love. To demonize electricity would be to demonize our beloved Water. At its source it is the same substance, the same molecules, simply restructured in a different molecular pattern. We saw our hypocrisy, how we rely on energy for our comfort and help ourselves to its gifts all the while vilifying its very essence. We protest *not in our backyard* and yet take freely that which benefits us.

The time is soon coming when technology will align with the harmonics of nature, but until this alchemical event duality reigns. All will become One. It is near. Patience. I think of the Ascension Key *Patience*—simply experiencing each moment as a gift with divine purpose—divine timing allowing for perfection to manifest. Patience is the balance of life force energy and Universal Law. When these two are in balance, it creates the harmonic union and intuitive Wisdom of Oneness of Self.

At the current level of our planetary technology this is the form electric power takes. Perhaps as we move into fifth dimensional societies there will be new sources of energy to sustain us, sources more appealing to our aesthetics and less dangerous to our bodies. But for now Water has freely given herself to the transformation of electricity for our benefit. Mother Gaia, through her daughter Rose Quartz, was showing us unconditional Love for all; showing us a new compassion for these transformers, showing us that all her gifts should be honored and blessed no matter what their disguise. We feel small for our belittling judgments which arose unconsciously. And then we knew why we were here—to make Peace with the power lines. And so with Peace Waters, Pleiadian Love Stones, Rose Quartz and prayer we blessed this sacred site.

## SHIMA AND SCOUT—FRIDAY MORNING
## STILL AT LAKESHORE

Lost in thought on this crisp mountain morning, Scout's whistle, our secret code of thirty years, brings me back to where I sit on the lakeshore. It rescues me from the stirrings of my mind and I look up to see *my* chipmunk. A year ago in the same spot I became sister to this chipmunk when she came and perched on my shoulder. Today she greets me again and we share a granola bar. I set aside my judgment of feeding animals "people" food and we enjoy our treat together.

We pack up our prayer blanket and belongings and begin the short walk back to the Chateau, our practice run completed. In the distance I hear the melody of the Native American flute wafting along with the shimmering sunrays reflecting off the water. In this state of omni-presence I am uncertain whether it is music from the realms of my subconscious or actually someone playing. Scout hears it too, so I know it is not a special etheric recital just for me. There on the steps leading into the lake is a lone hiker. From his bearded and bedraggled appearance it is evident he's made the woods his summer home as he wanders his path. He is playing homage to the sun's early morning majesty. I stop and perch myself on a rock to listen to this impromptu concert. Yesterday the harp, today the flute—what more magnificence do you have in store for us God?

## DUALITY ENTERS THROUGH THE HEART

Buoyed by sound and Light fully immersed in fifth dimensional Peace, we return to the Deer Lodge. Each encounter is an expression of harmony—the radiant rings of Light, the intimacy of the chipmunk, the musical magical flute. It has been an amazing morning. Back in our room we undress from our wooly early morning layers. The day will be hot once the sun fully rises. In the Rockies there can easily be five to seven weather patterns in a 24-hour stretch swaying the thermometer like a pendulum in a 40 degree swing.

This is not the place for cell phones and computers. If you are not wise to ecological etiquette the roaming charges will shock you into decorum. I have tucked my cell phone away at the bottom of my duffel. Even so carefully concealed, I do not fully disengage and simply leave it to vibrate. I am hooked. I am alerted by the vibration of an incoming text. Now I need to take a peak just to see. In less than a minute I forego the ensouling rapture of my present fifth dimension experience to engage in a third dimension text, putting God on hold to take this call.

The message reads: "Davids in emer w/poss heart attk. Pls say prayers n call in all healing angels. Thk u. lov. Candace." My eyes don't get past David. The only David I know is my daughter-in-law's brother. I leap to conclusions. My heart sinks. Here it comes, the chaos of August 5th, 6th and 7th we were told to beware. I have gone from full flight in the heavens to lower realm fear. Thud. I continue to read, bypassing the rest of the message and go straight to the signature line.

Who is calling out? An acquaintance. I have been pulled from our reverie by the collective consciousness of a blast text message. Tricked. I'm in the juice now. I can't simply ignore and delete, my ego would have none of that, so I share the Peace from our morning excursion and reply:

*We are at Archangel Michael's Temple in Lake Louise. Prayers are on their way. Everything is divinely guided. Surrender to His knowing and the gift will be revealed. Stay calm in the eye of the storm. David is loved and perfectly on his path. Faith and Trust will get you through. Peace All Ways, Shima.*

And we head to breakfast walking between two parallel realities. Free choice. What will it be?

We had big plans to hike to Lake Agnes hidden in a hanging valley high above Lake Louise. When we woke up, still tired from yesterday's excursion to Plain of Six Glaciers, the half-day, seven kilometer climb with an elevation of 1,204 feet sounded more grueling than great. We opted for gentle and serene. After breakfast the siren's call of Moraine Lake beckoned our return.

Banff National Park is a place where trails outnumber roads, where a car will only get you so far. We are so far north in such vast wilderness it is unsafe to venture too far off the marked trails. The remote terrain is inaccessible to most everyone except the avid alpinist. This creates clusters of humanity, cities of people all vying for the same trails, the same nature experience. Generally you find people and their activities sorted by their physical fitness. One usually finds outdoor enthusiasts outdoors, but here all types are seeking their once-in-a-lifetime nature experience, the young and old, children and teenagers, the infirm and immobile. Only the small children who hold the purest vibration are oblivious to the density trailing the tourists. Busloads of people embarking, debarking, time schedules, non-stop chatter, sudden starts and stops, bumping into each other. It's all here, all the things we go to nature to get away from.

The polarity is oddly curious in its stark contrast. It affects me. I try denying it, but I am bothered. I wish it were different. I do so want to be God perfect. It is easy for me to say "See God in every-one." Yes, easy when I think of it conceptually...alone by myself. And then I go out among people. "How many times, Lord Maitreya, did you show up at Lake Louise and I missed you?" You disguised. Me annoyed. I bring my awareness to you to *see* beyond annoying personality quirks and really *see* you—in every one. I wish never to miss those chances again. Make it easy. Show me *you* so I can *see* God in every one. He smiles I'm sure.

We stop at the headwaters, the end of the trail at river's edge. A wood observation deck stretches over the water. It is still early and we have the perch to ourselves so we settle in, feet overhanging the confluence of river and lake. I meditate. Scout contemplates. Soon there are people. I can tell with my eyes closed. The heavy plod of each foot jars the suspended platform. I open my eyes to see a man perched over Scout in search of a better view. Scout is trapped.

To this invisible cage the people come, tap on its bars, say a few things in a foreign language, then walk away as if we are simply part of the display. People walk over us as if they don't even know we are here. To one tourist Scout is nothing more than a human stump for the man to lean over. Scout has nowhere to go. It is very disconcerting and funny at the same time. We are starring in our own cartoon.

People stacked upon people, the small deck is now at capacity. So used to being part of the horde the individual is insensitive to personal space. In our Peace, in our silence we are invisible. I take my mala beads from my wrist and begin reciting my prayers. Out loud. On purpose. I've discovered people are uncomfortable being near praying people. It works every time. I pull out my journal and start reciting our prayer for tomorrow. The river's roar drowns my words. No one can hear. I read and pray. I focus. I ignore the people hoping they will disappear.

The cage of people loosens and Scout is freed. Between stanzas I reach over and whisper to Scout that the only place for solitude is in a canoe. Not true. Scout motions me to stop and look up. There, twelve canoes have congregated in front of us. Like bumper cars caught in the current, their oars are useless to the inexperienced. No doubt this congregation was drawn to the ascension prayer. Unknowingly their higher conscious keyed into the energy current and here they are before us wondering, "How did we get here and why?" We know. The clarion call went out.

## ROADSIDE PICNIC

Our schedule has no time. Mealtime is prompted by a break in the fifth dimensional frequency when our bodies nudge us into hunger. Late in the day after our delightful walk around Moraine Lake we seek out a picnic site. In this foreign country Canada, so similar to America and yet so unique, we discover under highway walkways leading to hiking trails. Not wanting the public to venture too far from the road, picnic tables crowd the roadside. People simply pull over, pull out their coolers, lay down their blankets and dine.

It brought back memories of our life in Portugal where umbrellas and family picnics dotted the roadside sharing space with passing diesel trucks and their trailing exhaust. We found it most peculiar that picnickers would perch roadside when the inviting landscape stretched beyond. Much like we think now. What we did not know is that we are guests of those who call this home and we share these roadside picnics with our hosts—the bears. When in Rome, when in Portugal, when in Canada—we followed suit and laid our blanket roadside, pulled out our cooler and dined. We were just getting used to this outdoor traffic tavern when our energy shifted. We've become attuned to a feeling in the air when a bear is near.

As you learned in *Journey OM*, I have not yet made Peace with the bear. It is a trigger for me, arousing a dormant fear I say I have transcended…until I feel the bear. My teacher, Mr. Bear, still holds a final lesson for me. He patiently waits the time when I will truly let go of all fear. Really, what would happen if I came face-to-face with him without the protection of the car where I safely ooh and ah-h at his regal stature? I reach for my animal guide and read that if the bear shows up, set clear boundaries and don't compromise. Be gentle and find answers to your questions. Go inside. Ask for what you want. The bear in the book sounds nothing like the bear I've contrived. Have I unfairly weighted the bear down with attributes he does not own? Was it Mr. Bear who taught me the beautiful lesson of *asking* which I share with you now?

## THE GIFT OF ASKING

It's not easy for me to ask. Maybe it's not easy for you, either. Asking brings up all sorts of issues and feelings in me—beholden, obligated, imposing. Perhaps you share some of the same feelings. I do not see an equal energy exchange. I feel I am asking and giving nothing in return. I discount myself, not realizing that possibly I am offering a gift by the simple act of asking. Unlike the feeling of power in being the *giver* bestowing gifts upon others when I ask I feel sheepish, demure, cowering. Asking makes me feel like the unworthy beggar.

*Until I realize*…asking carries a vibration of energy. I awaken to the *Aha* moment of the true meaning of *Gift Given—Gift Received*, the guiding principle on my pilgrimage. Does how we ask influence how and what we receive? Yes! If we ask with the energy of imposing upon others the person will feel imposed upon. If we ask with the energy of taking something then the person becomes wary of what he is giving away and becomes possessive and holds on. We both become restricted and the vibration shuts down the spirit of generosity in the person being asked. If we ask with the energy of not being worthy to receive we become the beggar giving away our power.

If our asking carries the vibration of opportunity to co-create, then our simple gesture of asking something of another gives the person the opportunity to expand their Wisdom by sharing their point of view. Asking becomes a beautiful form of giving an opportunity for more Grace. *Imagine if*…every time we ask for someone's help we express our request infused with the energy of offering them a gift—the gift of opening to the Grace of generosity?

What if every time we ask we are offering an opportunity to merge another's energy with ours and join the swell of energy created by collaboration? Our asking allows another's energy to ride the waves of energy created by a like-minded consciousness and move their projects exponentially into the field of possibility. In this view, is it not a sacred gift to ask from others? And if we ask with the knowing that we are giving as well as receiving, imagine the energy shift which occurs and the bountiful harvest we will receive from our requests? When I began to ask in the spirit of giving it changed me from the unworthy beggar imposing on others to the generous co-creator of expanding Grace. Now when I ask I carry the vibration of opportunity. It changes the spectrum of how I feel when I ask and how it is received. The stream of consciousness opens in co-celebration. Thank you Mr. Bear!

## BIKERS AND BEARS

We began to feel the Bear's presence. We hastily pack and head back through the culvert, grateful now that the car is so near. Emerging from the tunnel we see a temporary sign posted for the season: *Berry Season—Bear—Beware!* Our senses had not fooled us. Back to the car we see two bicyclists, a couple. This is high altitude country, lots of climb with little downhill reward. We jokingly remark that if they make it through this trip together it is true Love. We could think of nothing more grueling. The incline was at such a pitch that even in the lowest gear they were making no headway, prompting me to offer unsolicited advice under my breath "they should just walk."

They were pedaling so fast and making no forward motion. It was a steep incline and traffic was whirring by marring any sense of being in the great outdoors. Hot and miserable they had cast off their helmets and were either in a Zen moment (we hoped), or in a moment of proverbial hell. Then it got worse. A few hundred yards after we passed them, there, lumbering alongside the road, sharing the same path as the bicyclists, was a black bear. There was no escaping this encounter; their destiny had brought them head-to-head on the same path. Is this one of the few times when the droves of people driving by will be a blessing? We couldn't stop, turn around or warn them of their fateful meeting. We can only hope, as Velvet says, "These were two souls ready to meet the bear." Bikers and bears are unlikely companions and yet there will soon come a time when the lions will lay with the lambs and the bikers will share trails with the bears as soul companions.

The long day is winding down as we head back to the Lodge, what now feels like home after only a few days. This morning's dress rehearsal twelve hours earlier, eerily feels like another time zone. We'd traveled inter-dimensionally on the sun's first rays, were carried back to the time of Chief Joseph on the sound waves of a young man's flute, jolted into the third dimension by fearful texts, awakened by the scent of the trail and witnessed the unlikely encounter of bikers and bears. It was time to prepare for the purpose of our trip, opening the *Ascension Gate.*

We carefully pack our supplies for an early morning wake up: the ruby crystal bowl, the sacred waters collected at each stargate on Chief Joseph's trail, one large Pleiadian Love stone, the sacred bundle from our original journey, sacred ash and Chimayo soil—all neatly tied in a kerchief. How we would hold ceremony in the confines of a canoe would come later. Now we sleep.

Entrance to Tolo Lake

The boathouse at Lake Louise

Hiker with flute welcoming sunrise at Lake Louise

**My soul companion the Chipmunk**

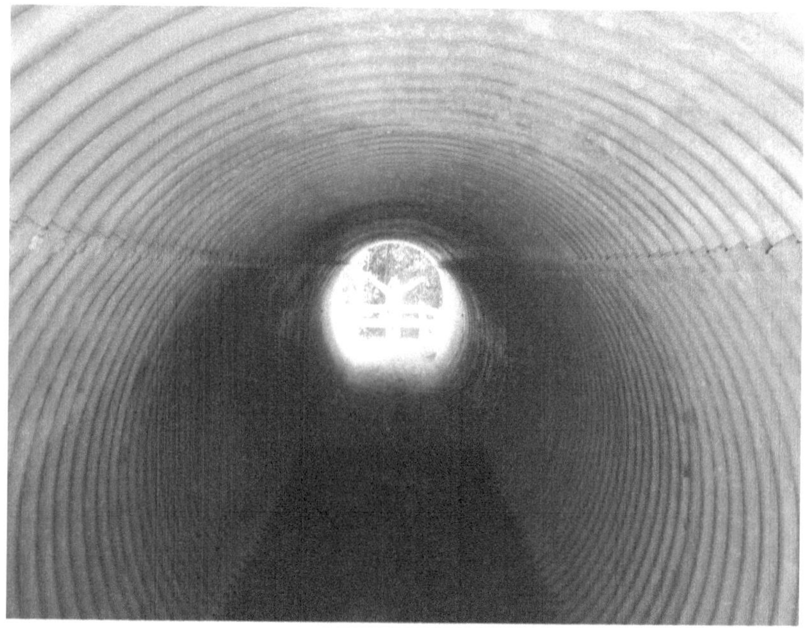

Entrance to our roadside picnic

Passage from my journal—Roadside picnic

# SATURDAY, AUGUST 8

## SHIMA AND SCOUT

*You will see a ring of light. Watch for it; you will know the signs. It may be a ring around the moon, a ring around the sun, maybe a radiant ring coming like a rainbow. It may be a ring of water that spreads from the center of a stone dropped in the lake. Look for the radiant ring. This is the sign when all of the ancestors and spirits of Peace will pray with you for the flowing of great abundance. This is the opening of the Ascension Gate when the sun's first rays strike the water on Lake Louise on the eighth of August. It is the re-creation of time before there was light when the ravens flew across the sky calling life and there was life.*

*As the sun strikes the water on this day Lord Sananda will ignite the Christ Consciousness into the heart of Mother Earth. This gift will be given at the Temple of Archangel Michael and will open the way for activations on Earth. Each time a ray of*

*Light touches water on this day it will re-create the original moment when the Sun brought life to Earth. This will happen everywhere on Earth beginning at sunrise at Lake Louise. Everything in a cycle has a beginning, a meeting point and a continuation. This is Lake Louise.*

I toss and turn, awaking every hour to check the time and finally rise well before the alarm. This is the first time in many months I can remember being on the clock. I had given up my watch years ago. I jostle Scout and together in our half-sleep we clumsily make our way from the warmth of our down comforter into the shock of the early morning cold. The mountain air is a constant reminder of the power of the planet controlling temperature, cold and hot, beyond the confines of comfort, never allowing us to forget who rules. I dress as though it is deep winter, layer upon layer, not wanting my sensitivity to the early morning chill to deter my mission. Packed and ready we head out while it is still dark.

When we arrive at the boathouse a short walk from the Lodge we are surprised to see twelve canoes already on the lake. At yesterday's sunrise there were but two, or maybe three. "Those who are called," I think to myself, and am reminded of yesterday's experience at Moraine Lake when tens of passersby on foot and canoe were energetically called to that moment in time to bare witness to a divine event. This full moon morning is a clarion call.

Two young college girls, Kiley and Gabrielle greet us. Corporately trained in customer service it was still not difficult to detect the admonishment behind their smiles. "You're late!" "We are?" "Yes!" Like a tour on regiment we have missed the departure time. Divine timing I think. Had we arrived earlier we would have been in the chaos of twenty-four people gearing up and pushing off. Their energy would have clearly shifted us into a different realm, not the sacred one we were entering. Divine timing was in play, making sure we enjoyed the early morning silence in solitude and allowing us to depart unobstructed well after the scurry of the group cast-off. This is God's schedule and people were kept at bay. We climb into the canoe, me in front, Scout in back, both facing forward. Hmmm…how's this going to work? The canoe is small, no room for error. I ask about the canoe's stability. I am assured of our safety by our guardians Kiley and Gabrielle—only two tip-overs and no rescues they boast.

We paddle out. It is serene. Cutting through the water, gliding effortlessly it's as close to floating, weightlessness and gravity-free as I can imagine. The sun still hides behind the mountain, but is beginning to light the sky. The waning full moon still has center stage. We row and glide, row and slide. We reach our destination and we're ready to begin.

I am reminded of the Nez Perce ancient custom of the Chief greeting his village when the first rays of sun burst over the mountains to light and warm the valley of winding waters. As Chief Joseph's delegate, I reenact this morning ceremony on his behalf as if he were here heralding the arrival of a new day: *I wonder if everyone is up! It is morning! Rise up! We are alive. Thanks Be! Look about! Go see the horses lest a wolf has killed one! Thanks Be! The children are alive! And you, older men! And you, older women! Also, that your friends are alive in other camps. Thanks Be!* In gratitude for the dawning of a new day Chief Joseph would then return to his lodge to a breakfast prepared with Love by his honored wife: serviceberry cakes, blue-black salmon, wild carrots and onions, roast fawn and kouse-gruel.

In the canoe, ever so slowly Scout directs my moves so I can turn around and face him without capsizing. He is skilled in the canoe. Talents surface I did not know. The required consciousness to maintain balance makes every moment mindful, thoughtful and sacred. How often do we rush through our actions unconscious of how we get from here to there? Scout uses his paddle as a serving tray and one by one he hands me the sacred supplies.

I play the ruby bowl. In Mother Earth's womb of water and stone the sound expands; a single note becomes a symphony. We are in tune, attune and begin our ceremony. By now the other twelve canoe congregants have made it to the end of the lake. We are alone to witness the first ray of sun hit water. We are to ourselves. We sit. There are no fireworks, no visible or audible signs of this etheric moment. Either I have internalized the opening of a stargate so completely that it has become one within me and I'm unaware of its occurrence or it is beyond my comprehension, too deep to access on the physical plane.

I look for physical affirmation but what we are doing is so deep it takes awhile to surface. Like the lake bottom, hidden from sight by the opaque glacier flour, there, unseen, until the silt has been sifted away. And then the moment we have prepared for arrives and the sun peaks over its hiding place and spreads its golden hue in a direct line from sky to Shima. I breathe. I inhale the rays of Light and color. I thank God for this privilege. The vibration is high. We have been calibrated to it and immersed in it for so long we do not feel its intensity. We know this feeling and in the knowing there is no feeling. It is All. It is everything. It is nothing. This is Peace. I am in the equilibrium of Peace. And in this place of equilibrium there is nothing outside of harmony opening to the fields of Love originating from the center of the Eye of God and the Heart of Mother. I am Peace and it is a state of unconditional acceptance of Self. I am in bliss.

## THE FEELING OF NO FEELING

Ah...feeling. It is an interesting and difficult concept presented for exploration on my path of enlightenment. To explain the concept of "no feeling" sounds like craziness and yet I know it to be true. I understand that to be in a vortex of all beingness has no wave lengths. It has no polarity. I am speaking of the realms beyond the third dimension and in Peace in particular, where there is only beingness. It is a difficult to verbalize.

Polarity creates the possibility and the need for an emotional response. When the division was made to experiment in the third dimensional element, judgment was a necessary ingredient along with duality. Joshua David Stone describes judgment "as discrimination or observation *without* Love." Spiritual discernment, unlike judgment, is an observation *with* Love. Developing the quality of spiritual discernment is essential to living spiritually on Earth. Joshua goes on to explain that we need to release thinking of "good" and "bad," "light" and "dark." There has to be polarity in the realm of duality but we do not have to attach *judgment* to "good" and "bad" "light" or "dark." As *A Course in Miracles* teaches, "There are no neutral thoughts. All thoughts have either an egotistical or spiritual charge."

We can learn to live a life without judging by practicing what Melchizedek calls the blessing system—to bless everything that happens in your life. Whatever happens in life happens for a reason and is therefore perfect. A person choosing the path of the negative ego is simply unconscious, living an illusion to learn a lesson, or teach us one. He/she is still the Christ, just not in their own thinking. This is their free will. As Master Jesus said, "Forgive them, Father, for they know not what they do." Sai Baba similarly teaches to welcome adversity by saying "Not my will but Thine, and, "Thank You for the lessons" to everything that happens to you.

The spiritual feeling I am talking about, the feeling of enlightenment is absent of emotion. And in that absence, like the surface of glass, nothing holds, the residue of emotion cannot stick, memories cannot form. This is the feeling of non-feeling. Our senses—the taste, the smell, the sight, the sound and the touch—all the joys of our senses remain without any of the attachment. The feeling is pure. It is God and it is enlightenment. It is the Freedom of feeling without the responsibility of a reply.

We believe that our *feelings* identify us and hold tight in fear that we may be less than compassionate, empathic human beings without the expression of emotion. To tell you that enlightenment is a state of *no feeling* stops the pages turning. For in truth, we all have *feelings* about our feelings. If you were to accept that feelings are tethers which tie you in emotional knots would you not cut loose in an instant? To imply that you will never feel again in an enlightened state contradicts logic. "What do you mean I can't feel? Feeling is what makes me loving, compassionate, caring," we tell ourselves.

I have held this concept of no feeling silent and sacred for just these reasons of resistance and craziness. I have searched for the words to describe the *non* of something and come up short. I know Freedom is a state of being, not feeling. Feeling is an emotional bond we create when we observe a rite, a ritual or an action—and then judge it. Emotions require duality and therefore only exist in the third dimensional realm. As we increase our Light quotient and raise our vibration we transcend beyond emotionally created judgment. Judgment is birthed of duality and polarity.

In the third dimension feelings are a way to connect person to person. When the emotional body still resonates with the physical form feelings are the necessary attachment to the race-mind consciousness. They are the anchor that keeps us in physicality. In essence feelings are the silver cord. We will arrive at a state of enlightenment when our contracts are fulfilled and our Light body is only interested in the higher dimensional forms. Then we will release our attachment to feeling, allowing us to freely transverse the Universe. For now, feeling is an emotional attachment of being human and is necessary to stay in the vibration of form.

To make someone happy or angry or resentful is ignited by the judgment of a situation. Even in the expression of Love we place conditions, then establish expectations and judge the outcome. We give and withhold our Love on how the person treats us, what they give us, if they are good to us. In the state of enlightenment there is no duality. It is All. It is everything. It is One. In this place of non-duality where judgments, and therefore emotions, don't exist, feeling becomes unfettered. It just is. Free. Unconditional Love describes this state of *no feeling*. To Love unconditionally there is no one, no thing outside of the beingness of Love. You can't *feel* it because there is no polarity to define it. Yes, "To say enlightenment is a state of no feeling sounds like craziness."

How do I explain Peace has no feeling? What the Masters do is observe the situation then move it into the highest state of consciousness without judgment. Those of you who meditate and have discovered the state of Samadhi understand.

In the beginning when I embarked on the stargate pilgrimage I underwent many vibrational shifts and initiations. I was physically and mentally aware of the transition. Now fully integrated, it has lost its unfamiliarity and has no feeling. Peace has no emotion, no feeling. Peace simply is. When one becomes One it goes without notice. A flower does not know it is a flower, a bee does not know it is a bee. It is simply a flower, simply a bee. All is All and All is nothing.

We remain suspended in this time warp, floating, gazing at the sunrise. I have entered the realm of being. *I AM* and as such there is no awareness, simply Peace. Peace is my soul companion.

## SHIMA AND SCOUT—SUNRISE—STILL IN THE CANOE LAKE LOUISE

Returning from this etheric moment after opening the *Ascension Gate* Scout requires a good row to the end of the lake to bring us fully back into our bodies. It feels good to use our physical strength in this rhythmic fashion. In perfect harmony, we cut through the opaque turquoise water. It is pure heaven, yet we don't identify it as such for it has become commonplace. I find I can't remember when it wasn't always like this. I ask Scout and watch him as he scans the vaults of his memory. I see the flicker in his eyes confirming, yes, he recalls those other times, but before responding, he passes this memory by his mind's reader board and replies that he can't remember either. I see in his eyes he still holds the memory of other times not so blissful.

## RESCUING THE RESCUERS

We begin our return. We are complete. We've handed over to God what it was we were asked to do as the divine vessels for His Will. Halfway back to the boathouse we hear the recognizable sound of an outboard engine. We're curious. No motor boats are allowed on this glacier oasis. In our reverie we only take notice of this out-of-place sound after it stops. Only in its absence do we hear. Like listening to the still small voice within, only in the silence do we actually hear. Off in the distance we see a boat, two people, standing with oars to the side. We gaze intently, but we're still too far to see. "Practicing rescue drills," Scout comments. Closer now, we sense they are stranded. I suggest we row over to see if they need help. Scout suggests, just like his response at Lenore on our stargate pilgrimage when the baby robins had fallen from the nest, "No, there's nothing we can do in a canoe. They know what they're doing. The hotel staff will assist them."

And in a replay of saving the robins I insist and we paddle over. "Kiley? Is that you?" I yell out breaking the silence. As the scene comes into focus we see two young women, stranded in a boat marked on the side RESCUE. Oars in hand they try to maneuver the bulky boat yet make no headway.

"What are you doing?" I ask.

"We're coming to rescue you."

"Rescue us?"

"Yes, because you didn't return with the others."

"Why would we return with the others?"

"The rules—you must depart together and return together by 7:30 a.m. When you didn't come back we came to get you, but our engine won't start and now we are stranded and we have to get back. Oh, you've created a terrible dilemma for us!"

Acknowledging their feelings, we make light of it trying to calm their anxiety, birthed more by embarrassment than fear. We ask:

"Do you have walkie-talkies?"

"Yes," they answer, "but we've left them at the boathouse."

I suggest we tie their boat to our canoe and row/tow them into shore. A chorus of, "No, no way!" resounds. I persist. Options are few.

"Let's just try."

Here were two inexperienced college girls with no training beyond handing out life jackets and reciting the rules. They were never expected to go beyond the dock. Now they're on their maiden rescue mission—being rescued. With only my Faith and their resistance, creating greater drag than the weight of the boat, we tie up and begin rowing. It works.

Once in motion their cloud of fear begins to lift. Scout and I are enjoying the adventure; the girls still too embarrassed to see the fun of their morning excursion. Safely back to shore we tip them handsomely for their troubles, apologize for causing them alarm, thank them for the adventure and say good-bye. The rescuers are rescued.

This scene held far greater significance than what appeared on the surface. We had just been given a visible sign of why we were called to open the *Ascension Gate* and I am reminded of why Chief Joseph was stopped at Bear's Paw unable to fulfill his prophecy.

*We as a people in 1877 could not go to this Ascension Gate because we lived in a world of survival, protection and refuge. When survival is no longer our focus and the way of Peace is at hand someone will lead the people to the eighth stargate, to the Ascension Gate (at Lake Louise), the place I could not go.*

## CHIEF JOSEPH—BEAR'S PAW MONTANA, 1877

Spanning four months and over a thousand miles, Chief Joseph, Chief White Bird and Chief Looking Glass had been outwitting and out-maneuvering the American Cavalry. Their Freedom and safety were in sight; just forty miles from the Canadian border. Refuge at the home of their ally, Sitting Bull beckoned. Yet Chief Joseph could not fulfill his destiny. His people were unable to rise above the illusion of the warring factions between the people of the First Nation and the new Americans. The dense vibration did not allow for Peace *or* abundance. Survival, refuge, hardship, scarcity—these mis-created forms of reality could not be transcended back in 1877. The race mind consciousness was too strong for Chief Joseph's vibration of Truth and Peace to break the cycle of survival.

Now in 2009, the collective consciousness has awakened to the higher vibration of Peace shattering the dense illusion that shadowed Chief Joseph. Now with the eighth stargate open, we are released from the limitations of survival, the need for protection, for safety, for rescue and can live our lives in Grace, in Peace and in Oneness. This is the *Ascension Gate* which opens all other gateways. There will be other ascension gateways throughout our local Sun Universe, but this *Ascension Gate* at Lake Louise at the site of Archangel Michael's temple is unique, igniting the frequency to remember the gifts of Love and Peace.

In their efforts to rescue us, the young dock hands entered the limited vibration of survival. Their engine was stopped. No rescue was possible in this higher vibration for there was nothing to rescue. All is Grace. All is divinely perfect. There is nothing to be protected *from.* Mankind's mis-creation and mis-qualified energy has been transmuted. Rescue boats simply don't exist in God's creation. With the boat engine stalled the *Ascension Gate* had been officially opened.

## SOUL PURPOSE, SOUL CONTRACT, DESTINY, PROPHECY, LEGACY

With the *Ascension Gate* open I pause to reflect on all that has transpired. The privilege of walking Chief Joseph's path and fulfilling his destiny humbles me. How blessed I am. How did I arrive at this sacred re-memoir of my divine purpose?

I awakened to my soul purpose in September 2007. I clearly understood why I am here—to live once again as a Christed being in a physical body; to fully embody my *I Am* Presence as Shima. I learned that each time we incarnate on Earth we choose a soul purpose which allows us to evolve into a higher echelon of Light and Love. There usually is only one soul purpose in a singular incarnation. It defines our destiny.

This one soul purpose however, may include many soul contracts. It's possible to complete the soul contracts we originally agreed to and accept new soul contracts in the same lifetime. This is my experience shared in *Journey OM, A Soul Journeyer's Adventure.* If we are successful in completing and integrating our chosen soul purpose in a lifetime it fulfills our destiny and then we will be offered greater opportunity to expand into a new soul purpose.

Think of an orbital system of the Universe with the soul as the sun. For every lifetime we have ever lived on the planet and every soul purpose we have chosen to create, the soul expands into multiple orbits as it vibrates into higher and higher fields of consciousness. This is how we expand God consciousness into greater fields of Love and Light on Earth. Each soul purpose becomes another ring around the sun expanding the orbit of the soul moving us beyond the physical, mental, emotional and spiritual bodies and into the five higher Light bodies—the Electromagnetic, the Epikinetic, the Eka, the Gematrian and the Zohar bodies.

When we have completed our personal soul contracts we can ask to individuate again and choose another soul purpose and destiny to fulfill the karmic pull of our unfinished past. Or we can decide to merge back into a unified field at our present level of evolvement and continue to expand into the five higher Light energy bodies. Every moment we live and breathe we are in training on some level or another. I have chosen to continue my ascension in a unified field. Moving from the finite field of my singular destiny to the infinite field of union allows me to be of greater service.

One lesson in the unified field is learning to absolve and resolve others of their unfinished karma. This gift of service quickens the Earth plane back into the unified field of God Source. What we do for others we do for ourselves. The well known, handed-down Wisdom of Jesus, "Love your neighbor as you Love yourself" and "Do unto others as you would have others do unto you" speaks directly to our love for others by transmuting their karma in the unified field. We are all One. Gift Given; Gift Received.

We live in an incredible time where everyone, without exception, is offered the opportunity for ascension. For millennia, ascension was not always so readily attainable or with so much assistance. Eventually everyone will return to the frequency of Love and union with God Source. Yet even with all of the guidance from the Spiritual Hierarchy we each must do our inner work and evolve our consciousness to meet the requirements for ascension. Through the gift of free will, some will continue to choose to experience separation. They are simply not ready for this evolutionary step. When they are, the Grace of ascension is available, for ultimately no one will be left behind.

On the Chief Joseph stargate pilgrimage I was offered a choice point outside of Chico Hot Springs, depart or remain on Earth. Both decisions had direct consequences. I answered with the desire to remain on Earth continuing to increase my Light quotient and to assist others in their ascension process. For my commitment to remain in a physical form I have been gifted with reuniting with great communities of Star Beings, sometimes consciously, most often not. Joining this community allows me to work in the unified field without the human drama of the third dimension. This is the concept of a *descended master—in* this world, not *of* this world. My acceptance of a new soul contract changed the course of my destiny, expanding my consciousness beyond the physical realm. This is the process of ascension to enlightenment.

When I write I joke, "Perhaps my prose is more suitable for our galactic neighbors to help them understand our *human beingness*. As my work finds its way into your hands you may concur with the truth in this possibility. When I realized that once we complete our individual soul purpose we can help others to evolve into higher planes (and at the same time increase our Light quotient) I became very excited. When I awakened to the knowing that I am an inter-dimensional soul journeyer with the ability to complete other people's unfinished karma and fulfill *their* destinies I became intrigued by this concept.

Not only intrigued but inspired and excited! I had been given a glimpse of my next soul purpose—me—fulfilling others' destinies which, for whatever reasons, were left unfulfilled. I sought to under-stand what the vibratory requirements would be if I were to tap into the higher ascended frequencies of other Masters who walked planet Earth and had not completed their destiny, just as I did for Chief Joseph.

How could this serve Mother Gaia and mankind as well as accelerate my own personal enlightenment? If I were accepted for this mission, to be a walker for Masters, it would require I carry a frequency in resonance with theirs. It would require I shed all illu-sion of my little self and step into my God Presence. It would require activation of the five higher Light bodies for they are essential to this pathway to God Source. Reminiscent of my prepa-ration before embarking on Chief Joseph's stargate pilgrimage I found myself back in training.

With passion and purpose I began a new journey. Initially, I sought to understand the meanings of soul purpose, soul contracts, destiny, prophecy, pilgrimage and legacy. I wanted to know how I could become an emissary for others who could not fulfill their destiny because they were no longer on Earth. And so with great fervor I went to work uncovering the meaning of the following key concepts.

**Soul Purpose** is defined as the soul's choice in a particular incarnation to create itself and expand into higher echelons of Light and Love. My soul purpose as an avatar of Peace is to descend the Councils of the Elohim who are directly related to creating Peace into the earthly realms of mankind's experience. As a disciple of Elohim Peace, I ignite the Elohim Councils of co-creation into the vessel of Mother Earth.

**Soul Contract** is defined as the agreement and commitment a soul makes to achieve his/her soul's purpose. My soul contract is to bring the Light codes of the Elohim Peace into physical form to be manifested from the densest aspect of consciousness into the full calibration of what is called the Zohar body.

**Destiny** is the chosen intention by an individual soul to enhance their evolution. The choice of destiny is determined by karmic lessons and qualified by the soul's vibration. When we are free of karma our destiny is complete and we can move into greater service. Destiny then moves from the finite field of personal destiny to an infinite field of unified destinies. When a destiny is fulfilled, meaning the soul purpose has been achieved by the completion of the soul's contracts, there is a choice: choose another individual soul purpose and personal destiny or merge back into a unified field at the current level of your soul's enlightenment and keep expanding. Destiny is the soul choosing a physical form or activity and merging all of its spiraling experiences into the expression of its greatest fulfillment.

A destiny is an individual's soul choice to accept the highest course the soul can see for itself at a point in time. The activity my soul chose was a pilgrimage. When someone says, "It is your destiny," it does not mean it has been predestined. It means that you have collected all the Light codes and Source energy to complete a soul contract in its entirety.

**Prophecy** is the combination of past, present and future magnetic frequencies forming into a grid that can be viewed as complete or fulfilled in the present moment even though it carries the magnetic frequencies of the future. In other words, the concept of a prophecy is reading the combined events of past, present and future occurrences and bringing these three time/space elements into the present moment as fête accompli. A prophecy is able to be foretold because this matrix already exists and is ready to be accepted by humanity. The form or activity of the soul might even have been prophesized. On a soul level when I agreed to a pilgrimage I was brought into the grid of that prophecy without regard to time or space.

In my personal experience, on a soul level I said *Yes* to fulfilling the prophecy of Chief Joseph's destiny by opening the stargates along Earth's gridline called the Chief Joseph Trail. My acceptance of my destiny happened long before I was cognizant on a conscious level that I was part of his prophecy. I could have consented to fulfill this prophecy eons ago, I just didn't know it. The person who says yes to a prophecy may, or may not, be ready for their part in fulfilling the prophecy, but the prophecy can be downloaded into the person and then the destiny begins. Time and space elements are not differentiated in fulfilling a prophecy. A prophecy is a vision that is held in time and *no time* and in *space* and *no space*. Prophecy is a completed vibration of a grid of intensity. A prophecy usually voices a destiny.

**Prophet** is one who can read a soul's destiny and foretell the moment when the magnetic frequencies align and the prophecy is already completed.

**Pilgrimage** is a journey following the path of a prophecy. When we combine our personal journey with a prophecy we raise activity from worldly exploration and become One with the highest intonation of the Spoken Word.

**Legacy** is a covenant between origins of family. Not origins of family in the biological sense, but a soul group that defines itself in a perfect vortex. A legacy is a covenant of a path. It is the stream of consciousness that completes itself in the family system one has chosen. In my example, I chose a legacy of Peace for my work. Other beings, Chief Joseph, Ghandi, Jesus the Christ, Martin Luther King and Nelson Mandela, also chose Peace as the vortex to enter into the lower realms for their work and their legacy. In that vortex of Peace I join with others who have the same legacy, the same origin of soul family. I am family with all who resonate with Peace.

Have you ever thought about your legacy? Who is your family of origin with whom you work to complete your destiny and fulfill prophecy?

## THE DIVINE RAYS AND SACRED FLAMES

The concept of legacy ties in neatly with the divine Rays or sacred Flames. Families of origin are beings sparked of the same divine Ray. I am sparked of the first Ray. The first Ray manifests the principles of omnipotence, protection, Faith and the Will of God through the power of the Father. The first Ray represents the initial impulse where thought-forms born of the Heart and Mind of God are given Life.

The chohan of the first Ray is Master El Morya. Archangels Michael and Faith and Elohim Hercules and Amazonia are of the first Ray. The color associated with the first Ray is blue and the corresponding stone is sapphire.

We can think of the Ray of which we are sparked as our inherent genius. There are seven divine Rays and each Ray corresponds to one of the seven days of the week, the seven notes on the musical scale, the seven main chakras, seven main endocrine glands, seven main organs and systems in the body. As do all things in our Universe and beyond, the Rays expand ad infinitum, but for this discussion I am speaking only about the seven Sacred Flames. An excellent source for learning about the Rays and Flames is Aurelia Louise Jones' book, *The Seven Sacred Flames.*

An enlightened being is one who has mastered each of the seven Sacred Flames. Typically when we incarnate, we will choose one or two of the divine Rays and through our life lessons we will master the God principles of those Rays in that lifetime. Sounds like choosing our destiny, yes? Our life lessons evolve around the mastery of the Rays, in other words "following our destiny."

Personally, in this lifetime, even though I am sparked of the first Ray, the Will of God, I chose to dedicate my learning to the mastery of the sixth Ray, the Flame of Resurrection. The sixth Ray is the activation of the I AM Presence. The chohans, or lords of the sixth Ray, are Lord Sananda and Lady Nada. Uriel and Aurora are the Archangels of the sixth Ray. Elohim Peace and Aloha are the architects of creation manifesting love through spiritual worship and selfless service.

The corresponding chakra is the solar plexus and the colors are purple and gold. The energies of this Ray are amplified on Thursdays. As a disciple of the sixth Ray, Lord Sananda is guiding me in my ascension through the Office of the Christ. Once we have mastered each of the seven divine Rays we are ready to expand the consciousness of God Source through our creativity and service. In other words, using the same definition of destiny, "once we have fulfilled our destiny we can move from the finite field of a personal destiny to an infinite field of all destinies and into greater service."

The sacred Rays we choose to master in a particular incarnation connect us to others who have chosen to master the same. Sounds like joining others in a legacy of common purpose, yes? Upon mastery of all the divine Rays we become candidates for ascension. This is our pathway to enlightenment and time for us to consciously seek the assistance of an Ascended Master for our ascension process. An

Ascended Master partners with a physical being to conduit his energy and carry out his God service for mankind. This is the exchange of energy and the commitment between Master and chela. The Master/chela partnership is approved by the Karmic Board and with all parties in agreement we become the Master's disciple and begin our ascension in earnest.

I am the chela of Lord Sananda. This is a responsibility of extreme commitment and dedication for both of us and a decision of great consequence. Lord Sananda is responsible for the energy he invests in me. If I fall short Lord Sananda must make up for my energy deficiency. In return for his assistance in my ascension, I am his conduit for service on Earth. Gift Given; Gift Received.

*Aha!* In this moment I am gifted with a revelation. I see how the study of divine Rays and sacred Flames is the same study of destiny, prophecy and legacy. I see how we can interchange the words *destiny* and *mastery of the Rays* to mean the same thing and understand the same principles. All of sudden I am aware that the ancient mystery schools, spiritual scholars and new age schools of thought are complementing each other, saying the same thing in different words. No matter the frame of reference we may resonate with, or in what school we gain our knowledge, we receive the gifts of divine Wisdom. We are transcending the language barrier and discovering that all of the Wisdom of the Universe is available to us in whatever package we choose. *Aha!*

# THE FIVE LIGHT ENERGY BODIES

One of my first lessons when I embarked on my path to enlightenment was to learn that our physical body is only one of four bodies that comprise our being. If you've been on your spiritual path you are familiar with the most common used terms for the four lower bodies—the physical, mental, emotional and spiritual—each with their own *health* issues, and each playing an integral part in our becoming whole and One again. Nearly all health problems, no matter how they are defined by the medical establishment, are caused by lack of harmony, imbalances and past or present unresolved issues in the emotional body. For the body to return to health, the deep seated feelings that initially caused the disorder must first heal. When harmony in the emotional body is restored, healing in the physical body becomes permanent.

We understand that our emotional and mental health influence our physical health. The fact that meditation and spiritual practice can improve our well-being is acknowledged, albeit reluctantly, even by the diehard dubious. These once *out there* concepts are no longer limited to new age beliefs. Even traditional medicine recognizes that our emotional state and stress levels play a part in our physical health.

On my spiritual path I healed, released and integrated every known and unknown malady affecting me from this lifetime and beyond. Just when I thought peeling the infinite layers of the onion would never end, I awakened to the truth: "I AM perfect just as I AM." *I AM* a divine God being whole and complete. And the healing and releasing ceased and I merged bodies—physical, mental, emotional and spiritual. And I felt good. The unique color spectrum of each of the seven chakras merged into a column of pure white Light. Yet even in this union of the four bodies there was a prompting nudging me into thinking...*there is more.*

And then I discovered that these four lower bodies are just that—lower planetary bodies. With the physical, mental, emotional and spiritual bodies in harmony, the next rung on the ascension ladder was not so far out of reach and I stepped into greater awareness, greater Love and Light; discovering there *is* more—the five higher Light energy bodies—Electromagnetic, Epi-kinetic, Eka, Gematrian and Zohar. Oh my! Vehicles of divinity!

Once I *knew* in my body, mind and soul that *I AM* just as much a part of God now as I ever will be all I had to do was cultivate this knowing. This is Self-Realization and the five Light energy bodies are the pathway to the higher realms beyond our experience of life on Earth. The five Light energy bodies are only attainable after the four lower planetary bodies have merged into one and are fully unified. There are no *absolute* definitions to define the five bodies for they are beyond this dimension. Abstract concepts, which might be helpful to you, only confuse me.

The easiest way for me to understand the five Light bodies is to compare them to concepts I know so I turned to Joshua David Stone's work with light quotient and DNA strands. His explanation took me only so far. To calibrate Light as a percentage, or even as a number of DNA strands, brings Light into a linear form. It's not. Light is a spectrum. Then I tried envisioning taking on the garments of the Light bodies as a series of initiations. This is more accurate. I could imagine an initiation being a conception point for accepting and holding higher levels of consciousness and at the newly attained frequency one of the Light bodies could be activated. The baptism of water is an initiation of purifying, cleansing and clearing and can be considered the conception point to the electromagnetic and epi-kinetic bodies; the baptism of Light and Holy Spirit activates the Gematrian body. I pieced together information remembering a body cannot maintain its physicality at 24-strand DNA; the Light simply moves too rapidly to hold shape. I know that the two higher Light bodies, the Gematrian and Zohar are activated and can be fully accessed when DNA reaches between 20 and 24 strands. Is it impossible, then, to take on the garment of the Zohar body while in physical form if it requires 24 strand DNA? Or, is this one of the gifts to us as divine human beings as *descended masters?*

First, it is helpful to define physical form. If we define physical form meaning the vibratory rate at which each cell can form an image and it can be seen by others, then yes, we have the ability to assume the Zohar body while on Earth. Is it a tangible body like I have now? No. At this writing I vacillate between 20 and 21 strand DNA. Before I can be initiated further I must stabilize my Light quotient. I am living life most consistently in my Eka body. There are short spurts when I am in my Gematrian body, but it is not constant.

We must personally experience taking on the garments of Light before their meaning is revealed. Through direct experience we become divine human beings free to travel inter-dimensionally while living in the third dimensional physical world. The concept of higher bodies must be experienced. The key to activating the five Light bodies is available to us all—a pure heart, an open mind and the willingness to awaken to who we truly are—our *I AM* Presence.

## THE ELECTROMAGNETIC BODY

The Electromagnetic body is the closest Light body to our physical body. It is the outermost form of the five Light energy bodies and the innermost form of the four planetary bodies, the spiritual body. Similar to the soul which is the connection between the physical body and the *I AM* Presence, the Electromagnetic body is the spirit connecting to the higher Light energy bodies. The soul includes aspects of the ego and the personality. It holds a persona which is a mask of illusion. The spirit does not. It is pure. The five Light energy bodies hold no distortion; they are spirit, not soul. The lower planetary bodies are soul not spirit. Until we move into spirit we cannot access the five Light energy bodies for we don't carry the purity of the vibration that is required. As we enlighten spiraling from the four planetary bodies to the five Light energy bodies we move from soul to spirit. The spirit is synonymous with the Electromagnetic body. It spans the entire spectrum of waves from the high echelons of the fourth dimension through the seventh dimension.

In the Electromagnetic body we have the potential to be God inspired. This is when I discovered meditation. This is when many discover the power of prayer. It was the first time I could consciously connect to the higher realms. Yet because the Electromagnetic body spans all frequencies fear kept me separate from my God Presence. I loved it and I feared it. I was willing to go only so far. I was afraid—of what?—that if I connected to this higher Light I'd get shocked like putting my finger in a light socket? It's easy to laugh now, after cultivating what I know, but my first experience with connecting with my Electromagnetic body hurled me right back into my limited consciousness…stuck in the familiar and comfortable. I realized through the merging of my lower bodies that there is more to what we see and feel in this dimension and my spirit wanted me to remember this. With Faith, my constant soul companion I surrendered to the unknown and the gifts of the Electromagnetic body immersed me in Light. Faith dissolved fear and the Light stream beckoned.

## THE EPI-KINETIC BODY

The Epi-kinetic body works with higher vibratory energy although still in the lower light realms like the Electromagnetic body. Every Light body that we don expands the field. It does not separate from the lower field. The Epi-kinetic body encompasses the dimensions four to seven of the Electro-magnetic body realms and expands through the twelfth dimension. Epi means to enhance and kinetic means energy. It is the body of high intensity, high vibration and motion. The Epi-kinetic body is activated by music, sound and vibration which stimulates the higher senses and inspires us into greater creativity. During the activation of my Epi-kinetic body is when I first discovered the sacred properties of the crystal bowls. "In the beginning was the Word, and the Word was with God, and the Word was God." The "Word" is sound, the source of creation. Tuning into the ineffable sound emanating from the crystal bowls awakened me to remembering Spirit.

Crystal bowls are made from pure crushed quartz crystal heated to 4,000 degrees Fahrenheit in a centrifugal mold. Each bowl is tuned to a note of the musical octave aligned with the chakras and the ascension keys. There are also alchemy bowls that combine gemstones and precious metals with the quartz crystal that create even more rarified frequencies enabling us to connect to the Five Light energy bodies. When we use the crystal bowls and connect sacred sound to our thought-forms and intentions we create a sound wave that matches the frequency of our thought intention at its highest calibration. The frequency of our mental thoughts is raised. When we add sound to our meditation we can open to higher and higher echelons of Light. The frequencies coming through the bowls add another dimension which creates a rarified field. Sound is expansive and vibrates through the cosmos for eternity.

I use the bowls to calibrate my body into a higher frequency and a state of openness I cannot consistently maintain in my present state of enlightenment. With regular practice I can integrate these higher vibrations as an everlasting vibration of my Light spectrum so I continually increase my constancy of Light. Oftentimes, before I begin writing I will play the bowls. It opens me to a very elevated state for my spiritual work and allows pure Wisdom to flow through me. I also use the bowls when I am feeling less than Light. When we are in a state of turmoil we can only vibrate to the level of Peace our bodies are feeling at that time. Peace is sidelined and anger, agitation and annoyance find their playing field. If I play the crystal bowls while I am distressed and focus on the word, Peace, the sound waves bring the vibration of Peace into higher Light forms and my body begins to resonate to the higher vibration allowing me to move back into the harmony of Peace. There is no place for turmoil.

The Epi-kinetic body is the initial experience of life beyond the physical body and it can open us to limited levels of contact with higher dimensional frequencies. If we are on the right frequency, we are able to change the physical form into the vibratory body (an advanced energy form) and then back into a physical form. Most exciting is that our consciousness travels with us. We can actually remember our experiences! We can experience the traits of the Epi-kinetic body—teleportation, levitation and materialization—through sacred sounds connected to thought-forms. The activation of this body is only for those who work with the Office of the Christ or divine Love. We must be selflessly pure of intent. Cosmic ascension and taking on the garments of the Light energy bodies is only granted once we have demonstrated we will not misuse these energies. We must be prepared to face tests and great obstacles to establish our mastery. We don't have to be perfect, but we must be sincere in our total service of Love, God and humanity. Beware of those who desire to use this power for mind control or have hidden agendas!

In the Electromagnetic and Epi-kinetic bodies I embraced the profound sweetness of *stopping to smell the roses*. And then once again I was nudged to go beyond the profound beauty of this new-found worldly existence. It was not easy for me to leave this feeling of bliss after experiencing scarcity, lack and suffering for eons of time. I discovered concealed behind the veil of *sacrifice* is the endless bounty of God's limitless gifts. In choosing God I must be willing to walk away from *anything* at *anytime*. This statement became real the day I chose my Zohar body (more on that later). I called on my master, Lord Sananda to help release me from my attachments to the Electromagnetic and Epi-kinetic bodies. With my soul companions Faith and Trust to guide me I was ready to transcend the Electromagnetic and Epi-kinetic bodies and activate the three higher Light bodies: the Eka body, The Gematrian body and the Zohar body.

## THE EKA BODY

The Eka body is a body of many smaller selves manifesting multiple forms of expanded consciousness. It is a plural life form which goes beyond the physical atomic structures and cell division. The Eka body can work in multiple time zones and parallel realms simultaneously.

This description of the Eka body having many selves is similar to my understanding of the monad, when all soul extensions are in unity consciousness. When a soul extension comes into unity consciousness it is at a vibrational level of its own purity and holiness—immaculate. It is one, yet it has the ability to separate from the whole. A soul extension moves into a field of lower density in service to rectify mis-qualified energy or bring greater Light, and then returns to the whole—immaculate—uncontaminated by its descent. It is possible for a soul extension to move into a field to explore and reinvestigate a wound of a sub-personality or another soul extension. We are living multiple lives. When we open up a field of descension we are allowed to retrace the information in order to solidify it in an even deeper, more profound way. Before this makes you crazy, remember we are discussing *Light* bodies not *physical* bodies. Whew! Better.

J.J. Hurtak beautifully describes the Eka body:

*The Eka body is the orchestrator and each manifestation of its existence is as a musical instrument. You have within your physical body the sitar. You have within your upper throat the trumpet. You have within your heart the drums. You have within your higher mind an electronic symphony. The Eka body is the orchestrator of the many plus and minus relativities or musical scores that you can read, experience, or share with your fellow brothers and sisters when you are in harmony with the Divine Plan. It is*

*the ability to sing and experience all of the glorious wonders of the*
*Godhead in their many dimensions.*

The Eka body is when we start to consciously embark on our inter-dimensional work. I excitedly thought this was the spiritual work I had accomplished, transmuting all of the mis-qualified energy at Souls Knolls on the Chief Joseph Stargate pilgrimage and in the parallel time-line of the second dimension Pleiades. To me, my service perfectly described the Eka body's abilities. Not! It was only preparation and the forerunner for my Eka body work. It helped me to remember my higher calling and seeded the possibilities into my Eka body. I must continually remind myself that this is not planetary stuff. This is higher dimensional, pure spirit, undistorted Light. This is God work. The Eka body only explores the fifth through twenty-second dimensions. It does not work in the lower zones of separation, abandonment and polarization. The Eka body's work is higher dimensional work.

Back to my opening sentence: "There are no *absolute* definitions to define the five Light bodies for they are beyond this dimension. We must personally experience taking on the garments of Light before their meaning is revealed." Envision the richness of our lives where we live and experience the rapture, opulence and beauty of all dimensions fully consciousness as *divine human beings.*

## THE GEMATRIAN BODY

Our highest purpose as human beings is to bring Light into greater manifestation on Earth. Our physical bodies are the perfect vehicle to send and receive Light energy. The Gematrian Light body is composed of light geometries in mathematical perfection which are revealed in multi-colors and sound. The Gematrian body is connected to divine knowledge and prepares the physical body to merge with the Christed *I AM* Overself. We are awakened by the Holy Spirit to an All-knowing. This gift of the Gematrian body is a gift of Grace.

When the right words or the right circumstances appear we are immediately connected to the Divine. There is no doubt. We see and witness Light in full form. When our Gematrian Light body is activated we can inspire, heal and create with conscious knowledge. Having this vibratory body allows us to be receptive to, and hold many more dimensions of consciousness. A portal is opened and our spiritual vocation is revealed before us. In the Gematrian body we possess super human energies able to move physical objects by sheer thought and even control the aging process. These are the powers and gifts of the Gematrian body.

We can hold many different bodies in many dimensions. It is not all or none. Soul extensions evolve at their own pace, some further along the evolutionary path than others. Some are firmly rooted in the third dimension and others in Universes we have no words to describe. For example, I know I have experienced times in my Gematrian body while in my Shima physical body, but I am not in my Gematrian body consistently. I function in my Eka body in many dimensions although there are aspects of me which have not yet given up the lower dimensions. Bit by bit the soul extensions holding me in a denser form will take on greater Light and I will live in greater constancy in my higher Light bodies.

There have been times in my meditation, in the garden and using my crystal bowls where, if someone were to see me, I would be glowing with rainbow energies around me. My heart would glow through my physical body and I would morph and shape-shift. What is seen as auras of Buddhas and halos pictured around saints is the Gematrian Light body. I have experienced this, although I don't have words at the moment to share with you the state of consciousness I was in. How can I explain weightlessness and intense universal genius?

Another musing…

I am trying to move away from using the duality-charged words "higher" and "lower" because they connote greater or less than. This assumes judgment and is not accurate. "Higher" is not better than "lower," yet it is so ingrained in my linear thinking it is a habit hard to break. I am practicing to think and speak spherically, not linearly.

If we consider the innermost center point of the circle being God/Source, the Ineffable, then the word "innermost" replaces "highest." Moving out from the center point of the circle, "inner" replaces "higher." As dimensions expand outward in my limited way of speaking, "lower" becomes "outer." "Outermost" would be the "darkest" realms of Chaos and the Underworld. This practice may seem trifle and insignificant, but this is how it is when we move into the finer and finer rarified realms and learn a new language which carries the "higher" frequency Light codes. There I go again! Practice will make perfect.

## THE ZOHAR BODY

The Zohar Light body is the manifestation of the greatest Glory and Love. It is the innermost of the five Light bodies. Unlike the Gematrian body which is seen as mathematical and geometric perfection emanating multi-colors and sound, the Zohar body appears as a flash of Light. When we take on the garment of the Zohar body we have become the resurrected Christ.

Immediately upon learning of the Zohar body I knew it was my calling. I have unknowingly yearned for this from the early age of nine. However, up until now my yearning was rooted in wanting to separate from some of my last duties of karma and not offer the service I am called to render. I wanted to escape. I was seeking Peace but it was individualized Peace—not collective Peace. I am not in any form of avoidance now. I am fully engaged in my true soul contract to bring the seed creation of eternal Peace to the planet. My yearning is no longer an individualized choice, but a much more expansive one in service to the collective universe. With this shift in perception my ability to serve in a greater capacity in the Zohar body is now possible. I ask for this daily. It is my greatest desire, although even in my yearning I hold constrictions—the greatest being my love for Scout.

Before now the Zohar Light body has only appeared on the physical plane a few times in history. It is possible. The Ascended Mother Gaia now maintains the increased Light and vibration necessary to bring this opportunity into full possibility in 2011. Many of us will be the way showers learning how to move ourselves into these bodies. It will have an enormous ripple effect and more of humanity will be able to do it. There are several monasteries in Tibet where many have moved into this field of existence, learning and practicing. It is an extraordinarily ascended state. The physical form is not how we perceive it.

The Zohar body can be seen because the vibratory rate of each cell has the ability to form an image. It is not a tangible body like we have now. It holds much higher electrical Light and Love than a physical body could ever hold. Every Master who has reached the Zohar body has brought in a physical holographic form so that people could be with this Master and be taught by him. But they could not fully embrace the Master in a physical form. He did not live, eat and drink in the same way we do. Once we move into our Zohar body we will not be able to live and function and breathe as we know it. Our bodies cannot be touched or fed. They will be in a form we could call ghost energy. It creates a shimmering Light body which moves in and out of form but is not solid. In essence others will *feel* us, but not be able to physically hold us.

The best example, of course, is Jesus when he received his Light body and became the Christ. People could see an image of him such as a holograph is seen. Was it tangible? Could he be touched? Could he be fed? No. I am on the threshold and capable of holding the Zohar body while still being on Earth continuing my service. If I choose this next step of enlightenment it will not be a tangible body as I know it or as those who love me know it. Its frequency will simply be too high to be contained in the material world. We use the Zohar body for ascension and descension activities. Yes, we are a physical body, but when the Zohar body is activated we function as multiple spiritual bodies in many dimensions and Universes simultaneously.

When the five Light bodies are linked we can bypass the physical laws of the material Universe. When the Zohar body is aligned with the fullness of the Christed *I AM* body, it appears and we spiral into another level of evolution, into the arrangement of the Six Bodies, the five Light bodies plus the Christ body. We move into a level of cosmic participation where we are empowered with the fullest Glory. The head, the heart and the crystals in the hands and feet become the radiant presence of the Elohim and we carry the Divine Image and Similitude within us. Our consciousness changes and we cease functioning as a singular body and unite with the body of the Universe as a whole. This is Oneness.

When the opportunity to take on the garment of the Christ body entered my consciousness as a genuine possibility, my mind and ego started reeling. Am I selfish to want self-fulfillment at the cost of Scout's sorrow and Jimmy's, Liz' and Micah's perception of losing me? Am I of higher service to live in this body and vibration in which I now dwell? Is this my will or Thy Will? What responsibilities are tethering me? Do I have any undone business? Are my contracts complete? Is there anyone or anything I am unwilling to surrender to assume the Christ body?

The question is: Can I bring myself into greater Peace fulfilling the purpose of all that has been intended through me in my acceleration of Spirit in physical form and then move out of physical form to hold that consciousness consistently? Hmmm, I am ready to be fully encompassed in the consistency of my essence.

What I do know is self-fulfillment is never selfish. No Master has ever allowed the aspects of another human to stop the evolution within them. Nothing will stop a Master's spiritual journey to be a fully realized cosmic Christ, nor will it mine. Will Scout be sad? Perhaps; Yes. But Scout knows my path, my desires and my calling. He knows his soul contract and the agreement we have together. He knows it is my soul purpose to bring myself into the design of my divinity. In our thirty-five years together our soul contracts have been an unspoken agreement between us, ones that surface occasionally in poetry and musings, but always a prospect in the future not to be considered now. The time is NOW. Will I say *Yes?* Will I be here in physical form when this book is in your hands?

With this information of the Zohar body I made the conscious decision to fully embark on this path. *Whoah!* Here's what happened. Every un-reconciled aspect of me surged forward. Those soul extensions, mine and my soul group's, which had been along for the ride hidden in the ethers, surfaced. Once again trials and tests appeared. Could I stay in Love and Light? Could I love these "less than loveable" aspects of me? Can I be the worthy disciple of Lord Sananda and follow the Way and the Word?

Situations presented themselves—one after another, too rapid to recall. I'd say I failed, but in spiritual reality failure doesn't exist. All is perfect. All is a gift. Lessons learned. But it felt like failure. For days I dwelled in remorse for my actions I thought noble. My emotional body lagged behind still trapped by the need for approval and Love. Unworthiness hurled me into a pit void of self love. After four days of this, working with the crystal bowls, journaling to Lord Sananda and a trip to my gifted friend Gabrielle to be energetically dusted off, I slowly returned from the abyss. My mettle was strengthened, my self-love restored and the path of Thy Will made clear. This is my journey, silent and sacred, only mine. It does not matter when, where or how. When I am ready it will be in a holy instant. I am on the path. I have said *Yes.* I have relinquished all earthly responsibility. Every step I walk through life I bless, pray and give Light. It does not matter the results of my books, my Peace Waters or other services. What matters is to give Light in every moment. I am a soul journeyer seeking Source/God/Mother/Father/All That Is. Gift Given, Gift Received.

Heaven on Earth—As Above-So Below
Lake Louise, August 8, 2009

# IN SCOUT'S WORDS

Only a Memory
I awoke this morning
With the warm sunlight on my head
Reaching over to touch
Opening my eyes to see......

Only a Memory
I went for a long walk today
All the way to those cliffs
To celebrate and kiss.....

Only a Memory
Photos may fade and tatter
The years go by without matter
But I can see it as if it was today
And cherish it so
Even though it's…

Only a Memory
It was four years ago today
I remember her say
She has four years left
And then she'll be going away
Now I'm here to stay
With…

Only a Memory
As I turn down the lights
Resting my head to sleep
I wait patiently to dream of…

Only a Memory
My eyes swell shut
My throat chokes up
When I look to see
Myself alone
Thinking about…

Only a Memory

## SHIMA AND SCOUT—SATURDAY MORNING
## ASHORE AT LAKE LOUISE

Returning from this musing, these moments in the classroom of the *School of the Wisdom of Faith,* we are back on shore. Having said our good-byes to Kiley and Gabrielle we take a final walk from the Fairmont Chateau to the Deer Lodge to pack and go. We're solidly grounded; grounded *in* and *out* of this world. The veils have been lifted; jumping timelines and traversing dimensions seem commonplace. We go through the motions of packing and checking out, but we're not really there and if we're not careful we'll find ourselves in a parallel reality. This is stuff of science fiction and we're in it—both of us.

Stepping out from the Lodge we are met by three ravens. Something is different. They are circling our departure in an unfamiliar pattern. They are singing a new song—distinct and beautiful, not the typical caw. They swoop low to make sure their celebratory dance will not be missed. Chief Joseph tells us the ravens are the bringers of the dawn. *This is the moment of creation when the sun first strikes the water and the ravens fly across the sky calling life. And there was life.* And now the ravens in reflection of those original times christen the opening of the *Ascension Gate.* These black-winged soul companions have choreographed their fanciful flight perfectly for this ascension celebration. We *Journey OM.*

Sunrise—Lake Louise—Saturday, August 8th

**Scout reflecting—The Ascension Stargate is open**

**Mission Accomplished!**

Passage from my journal

**Heart to Heart—Reflecting Oneness**

# MONDAY, AUGUST 10

## SHIMA BACK IN WHITEFISH

We have been home in Whitefish for two days and the journey continues. It is 2:16 a.m. Consciousness creeps into my sleep. For sixteen minutes I have resisted the prompting to get up and write, but its constant nudging will not relent and I now have pen in hand. I startle at the thought that I have not been journaling. Oh my! Will I forget? Why haven't I been writing? Fully awake now, intent on chronicling this supernal experience, I begin to pull the bits and pieces from my memory. Some things are so deeply embedded they take awhile to surface. Much like the water of Lake Louise this time of year, opaque with glacier flour, much of what happened is shrouded until the silt has sifted and settled. Now, in the early morning hours, I put pen to paper and ask for clarity in sharing my story with you.

## PROPHECY SPEAKS

*You can expect chaotic times in the days prior, August 5, 6 and 7, leading up to August 8th. There will be earthquakes, storm fronts, chaos in warring countries and sectors of people who will leave the planet. These events are to be seen, not as catastrophic loss, but as expressions of correcting disharmony.*

Words shared months prior. Back when—before—they had no context or meaning. Now a glance at yesterday's news headlines and this past forecast is remembered.

*Nine Die in Helicopter and Plane Crash Over Hudson River; Millions Flee China Typhoon; Dozens Missing in India Mudslide; Plot Foiled to Assassinate Indonesian President; Over 700 Fires Recorded in British Columbia—Two Towns Evacuated; 250 Inmates Hurt, 50 Hospitalized in California Prison Riot; 3 Women Killed 9 Wounded by Gunman at Pennsylvania Fitness Center; 8 Die in LA Police Chase Crash; 48 Killed and Hundreds Wounded in Iraqi Bombing Spree.*

There boldly in black and white prophecy speaks. This is one time where we would not ask for affirmation of the foretelling of chaotic events to occur on August 5th, 6th and 7th. I am reminded to observe these events as expressions of correcting disharmony and not view them as catastrophic loss. But still. The Bible says it took only days to create the Universe. How long did it take for humankind to mis-create it? And how long will it be to rectify our actions born of ignorance? The moment we become aware, forgiveness is given in a holy instant. We must wake up!

## SCOUT REVEALED

For the first time in three days, I see Scout naked and the memory of our hike to Plain of Six Glaciers comes rushing back. It is inscribed on his torso. His fatigue, his silence, his suffering. Odd that he concealed himself so well. Exposed now before me his entire trunk is afire in blisters and hives. Sometime after our soak at Radium Hot Springs he broke out in a rash. I can only imagine the ferocity of this intrusion at its inception. Three days had calmed its roar. It was painful to look at. I vicariously suffer the burning, the itching and his withheld fear not knowing what it could be.

"I didn't want to distract you," his feeble excuse.

Another gift of his selfless Love for me. Now I am in pain for him. To experience so much discomfort, in silence, for my sake opens my heart to more Love than it can hold. We each have our own way. With nothing more to conceal I inspect my beloved's body. Out of sight, one welt looks like the source, perhaps a spider bite. His secret revealed, I treat him with hydrochloride and hydrocortisone and guiltily throw in a few essential oils to assuage my feelings for foregoing the naturopath's way in the time of crisis. Intuitively I know this is a purging for Jim, a release, another step up the ascension ladder that prepared him for opening the *Ascension Gate*. I know that everything we experience is for our highest good. All is a gift regardless of its packaging. I know Jim's discomfort is a blessing and merits revealing. Still...

## KWAN YIN TO SCOUT'S RESCUE

Leaving nothing to chance, having seen the welts on Jim's torso, I schedule acupuncture appointments for each of us with Christi. While waiting for Jim I sit in the sun and enjoy this time to contemplate.

Christi is an integral part of my soul team, a healing master who assisted me in the transformation process from the carbon body to the crystalline structure. In the hands-on, reputable and recognizable healing art acupuncture, Christi adds legitimacy to my transformation. I can use this platform to share and help others understand this carbon to crystalline transformation. Archangel Metatron over-souls Christi; she works closely with many Arcturian metaphysical acupuncturists, all under the guidance of Lord Arcturus and Metatron. Her healing gifts are not limited to the physical body. She has the ability to treat all the bodies, spiritual, mental and emotional.

Working together we are able to identify out-of-step activities which detour us from our path. Once identified, we can transmute these missteps before they manifest ailments in the physical body. Christi acts as my transceiver and together we are downloaded with intuitive Wisdom to expand our God work. In our acupuncture sessions I am being trained by the Masters. Questions I ponder are revealed to me. I get a word, she gets a word, and together we create a story line through meridians and acupuncture points. Her insights trigger my intuition and together we help each other connect directly to our God Presence energetically creating a trinity—Christi, Shima and Source.

Today we understand the greater import of the spider bite on Scout. The spider bite was a gift, yes, in disguise, from Kwan Yin. It is only natural it would be Kwan Yin who would mentor Jim. He is very connected to her compassionate energy. She is the divine feminine deity who first reached into Scout's subconscious and awakened him to the splendor beyond the veils. Her statue graces our home emanating Mercy and Compassion. She is fondly called the Holy Mother of the East. She is known as the Goddess of Mercy; Mercy—the simple giving of more assistance through Love than earned through merit. Kwan Yin served mankind in China, going back millions of years when the Ascended Masters walked freely among us in the golden age of Peace and harmony, long before the fall of man. She held court in the Temple of Mercy and assisted her people in the mastery of energy and the fulfillment of their Divine Plan.

Using the Violet Flame Kwan Yin would mercifully transmute karma before it could externalize as distress to the soul, mind, body or worldly affairs. We all have our Masters guiding us on our way. Scout's is Lady Master Kwan Yin teaching him the way of the divine feminine, the divine Mother's Love. Kwan Yin used the spider to rectify and purify Scout's masculine archetype at the root, opening the way to the divine masculine.

It was no coincidence that the rash flared at his root chakra, the first chakra—survival and the source of physical creation, and the second chakra—the source of his masculine identity. Scout is being prepared to carry and express the perfect balance of the divine feminine and divine masculine in his body which is all part of his soul purpose and contract fulfilling his destiny. Many initiations will be required for him to integrate this divine androgynous vibration. This is the beginning if he freely chooses. The misdirected male archetype rooted in the collective consciousness; the archetype which arrogantly controls, dominates, and manipulates will be transmuted from his cellular memory, both in his physical body and from past incarnations. Had Kwan Yin not intervened with the spider bite a major illness was possible to release him from this archetype. Mercifully, this aggravation was much less painful than what could have been. Once Scout has fully integrated the divine masculine, he will be able to assist in transmuting the mis-qualified male energy held in the race-mind consciousness. This is his destiny and will be his gift of service. It will come much later.

Like all of us, Scout must first experience transformation on a personal level. Once the mis-qualified male archetype has been transcended the divine masculine energy can be ignited. The other aspect of Scout's destiny is to open to receive the divine Mother's Love. Who would not wish to receive Love? And yet, we withhold and reject Love to create false protection to shield us from the deep pain of abandonment. Only by surrendering to our vulnerability can we open to Her Love.

Surrender is the key to all of God's gifts whether it be Love, Freedom or Peace. Chief White Bird and Chief Joseph faced the same paradox of surrender at Bear's Paw. Only through surrender could they be free. Contradictory to our soul purpose, we entangle ourselves in dual false illusions unwilling or unable to loosen the knots of our self-imposed safety net. Faith and Trust are the keys which open to surrender. Subconsciously, Scout was in great fear about this journey and opening to his divine masculine and divine feminine essence. To enter the *Ascension Gate* one can no longer have survival needs. Chief Joseph and Scout included.

The bite affected only Scout's two lower chakras, the root—survival—and the sacral—his masculine identity. Mother Nature was preparing him to receive his rightful gifts of ascension. This bit of aggravation gave him something else to focus on so he wouldn't be overwhelmed by the initiations. Kwan Yin intervened with the spider bite; the merciful, compassionate Mother's Love at work. In that moment he was in fear of the unknown and his fear was creating the potential for illness. Sometimes we subconsciously choose to *bottom out* or be *dropped to our knees* in order to see the Light. Instead Kwan Yin sent Scout the spider bite. Gift Given; Gift Received.

Kwan Yin watching over Scout

# Sometime in the Future

## Return to the
## Chief Joseph Trail

Jim is my Scout. He is my Love, my friend and my protector. He is an enormous gift to me and integral in helping me manifest my spiritual work. But God has greater plans in store for him. On this pilgrimage to open the *Ascension Gate,* Jim stepped into his own power. I see what lies ahead: Jim's purpose and destiny which only he can fulfill. In this moment of awareness, I knew we must return to Eastern Montana and retrace the final journey of Chief Joseph. Jim has received a tap on the shoulder; he has been called.

Circles within spirals, destinies within prophecies. I see the confluence of the Yellowstone and Clarks Fork Rivers where Jim will rectify the mis-creation of male energy and reclaim his masculine divinity. I see the Mussellshell River at the time of Chief Joseph a place of grassy meadows, lovely streams, trees and berries. After being on the path of scarcity this was a stopping place of nourishment for Chief Joseph's worn people. Here Jim will be nourished with unlimited Light. For Jim this is the divine feminine portal where he will fully embrace the divine feminine aspect in his planetary masculine body. Jim will experience and feel the feminine Christ consciousness enter his heart anchoring it fully in his physical body in masculine form. On our return trip to Eastern Montana Jim will be washed over with Love of the divine feminine energy. Once integrated into his being he will be able to carry this vibration outwardly. This is his destiny. He will feel the Love of Mother like he has never felt before. He will feel it as his own—at One—Self Love.

Jim's destiny is to reveal the perfect balance of the divine feminine and divine masculine to others by simply walking his path. In the simplicity of quietly being he will be a way shower for others. After this pilgrimage Jim will embody the feminine Christ consciousness of Lady Nada, the mercy and compassion of Kwan Yin and the strength of the Ruby Knight of Lord Sananda—all in equal balance. This is Jim's call to step into his *I AM* Presence. I will be his Muse, by his side to ignite the creativity ready to be released as we walk in partnership waiting for the next tap on the shoulder.

# WALKING FOR CHIEFS JOSEPH AND WHITE BIRD COMPLETING DESTINIES— FULFILLING PROPHECIES

There is more to be revealed. We will return to Chief Joseph's Trail and the stargate path. My soul journey to fulfill Chief Joseph's prophecy is not yet complete and Jim's pilgrimage is just beginning. Chief Joseph's and Chief White Bird's destinies were intertwined and only in the unraveling of the two will their souls be free to *Journey OM*. Will I walk their path from Freedom to Peace? Chief White Bird's flight for Freedom to Canada and Chief Joseph's surrender for Peace at Bear's Paw were in opposition. Chief White Bird believed to surrender would mean relinquishing independence. His fleeing to Canada in the name of Freedom asserted that surrender and Freedom could not be in the same vortex.

In truth, surrender is the key to Freedom opening the way to unconditional Love and ultimately Peace. It is an illusion to believe surrender is giving up. We are conditioned to believe surrender means to renounce Freedom. In our grip to hold onto the perceived ideals of Freedom we incarcerate ourselves in ideology. In truth, we can only realize Freedom through surrender. To let go of all attachments, to allow everyone their free will to choose, and to accept what is, give rise to Freedom. If we think of surrender synonymous with the Will of God, in this context, surrender is simply saying "Thy Will, not my will." There is a spiritual evolutionary spiral—Surrender—Freedom—Unconditional Love—Peace—circles within circles, like the rings when a pebble is tossed into the pond, ever expanding the emanations of the invisible worlds made visible. This is the externalization of the Light of God made manifest.

Surrender to the Will of God—Allowance for others' free will—Acceptance of all that is—in this place dwells Freedom, Freedom to Love unconditionally and live in Peace. Before Chief Joseph's legendary incarnation as the Chief of Peace of the Nez Perce, Joseph was already in the expanded state of consciousness of Peace and had accepted the Will of God to surrender at his moment of choice at Bear's Paw. Only in this state of enlightenment could he have carried out his destiny to seed the stargates. Choosing Peace through surrender at Bear's Paw was his ascension to the highest caliber of enlightenment. Chief Joseph—in Truth—chose Peace.

# *Epilogue*

We were called to Lake Louise. We answered the call and the circle and cycle of this adventure was complete. But the way of Ascension never truly ends, ever spiraling upward. Everything in a cycle has a beginning, a meeting point and a continuation. This journey to Lake Louise was the culmination of opening the stargates for Chief Joseph and the conception of the New World of Peace. We opened the eighth stargate, the *Ascension Gate*, making the way for whoever chooses to follow.

In November of 2009, Scout and Shima were called back to retrace the last miles of the Chief Joseph Trail in eastern Montana; their mission to align opposition with apposition. The frigid, wind-whipped, barren expanse did not welcome their efforts. There would be no comfort in their quest. The collective consciousness was unwilling to reveal this paradox or relinquish control. For the final fulfillment of Chief Joseph's prophecy it would be essential to repair the rent in the fabric of Peace and Freedom. And so Shima and Scout returned.

For aeons the masculine archetype has misused its power in suppressing the divine feminine aspect of our total being. As emissaries of Chief Joseph and Chief White Bird, Shima and Jim will join all the Ascended Masters and Emissaries of Light who are dedicated to the ascension of Mother Gaia, her kingdoms and mankind. Bringing into balance the divine feminine and divine masculine, unifying the consciousness of Peace and Freedom and fulfilling the destinies of Chief Joseph and Chief White Bird will be their charge—in essence, merging Heaven and Earth. The delicate balance must be restored. The time is NOW. The prophecy continues. November 2009 is the date. To be continued…

Book III of the *Journey OM* Series.

**God's Work Is Child's Play**
*Journey OM*

# REFERENCES


Andrews, Ted (1993) *Animal Speak.* United States: Llewellyn Worldwide Ltd.

Ahsian, Naisha (1995) *The Crystal Ally Cards.* East Montpelier, VT: Heaven and Earth Publishing

Farmer, Steven (2006) *Animal Spirit Guides.* United States: Hay House, Inc.

Hurtak, J.J. Ph.D., Ph.D. with Desiree Hurtak, MS. Mc. (1994) *The Five Bodies.* Los Gatos, California: The Academy For Future Science

Jasmuheen, **www.jasmuheen.com**

Jones, Aurelia Louise (2007) *The Seven Sacred Flames.* (2004) *Telos—Volume I.* Mount Shasta, California: Mount Shasta Light Publishing

Moore, Judith K., www.recordsofcreation.com

Myss, Caroline (2007) *Entering the Castle.* New York, New York: Free Press, A Division of Simon and Schuster, Inc.

Nerburn, Kent (2005) *Chief Joseph and Flight of the Nez Perce.* San Francisco, California: Harper San Francisco, a Division of Harper Collins Publishers

Papastavro, Tellis S. (1972) *The Gnosis and the Law.* Tucson, Arizona: New Age Study of Humanity's Purpose, Inc.

Schroeder, W. (2005) *Ascended Masters & Their Retreats.* Mount Shasta, California: Ascended Master Teaching Foundation

Simmons, Robert and Ahsian, Naisha (2007) *The Book of Stones.* East Montpelier, Vermont: Heaven & Earth Publishing LLC

Stone, Joshua David (1998) *The Easy-To-Read Encyclopedia of the Spiritual Path, Volumes, I, III, IV, VI, XI, XIV.* Sedona, Arizona: Light Technology Publishing

Tolle, Eckhart (2003) *Stillness Speaks.* Novato, California: New World Library, and Vancouver, Canada: Namaste Publishing

Wilfong, Cheryl (2006) *Following the Nez Perce Trail.* Corvallis, Oregon: Oregon State University Press

Williamson, Marianne (1994) *Illuminata.* New York and Toronto, Canada: Random House, Inc.

# $I_N$ $G_{RATITUDE}$

*The Journey OM* series is the collaboration of many gifted individuals and spiritual masters coming together to record this story of the timely and powerful awakening to our ascension process. Grace brought us together. In Gratitude I share the co-creation of the *Journey OM* series with you.

**Mike Clark, Montana, artist and brother.** Rare is the gift of taking words on the page and transforming them into visual images that transcend the limits of the mind. This is Mike's gift. Thank you, Mike, for creating the covers that inspire readers to open the pages of *Journey OM, A Soul Journeyer's Adventure* and *The Soul Journeyer's Companion.*

**James Gordon Kelly IV, "Jimmy," artist and son.** Inspired by Chief Joseph, Jimmy captures the Chief's highest vibration in the full mastery of his ascension. Jimmy's gift is the visualization of Creation—the ability to draw the frequencies of Light into his artwork, most notably in *The Ascension Keys,* where symbols and images are gifted to us for acceleration on our Spiritual path.

**Teresa Brady, my friend "T".** Teresa is my professional editor, Starbucks pal, and the friend I count on for honesty and clarity. Teresa's encouragement to "let it see the light of day" when it would be easy to hide it away has brought this tale forth.

**Judith K. Moore, visionary, mystic, oracle, and friend.** Judith's dedication of service to the awakening of Heaven on Earth is unwavering and a blessing for us all. Through Judith's insight I was able to unite with my God Presence and open to my destiny of fulfilling Chief Joseph's prophecy.

**Jim Kelly, my beloved husband, companion and Scout.** Together we journey heart-to-heart in love, laughter and awe. Through Jim's eyes the indescribable beauty of life continues to unfold. His gift of poetry and photography light up my words on these pages. *The Soul Journeyer's Companion* and the *Journey OM* series is our love story in more ways than One.

My special thanks to **Jeff and Jenn Eckert** for their publishing expertise. Their text layout and design make it easy on the eye and a book to behold. And thanks to the talented team behind the scenes; everyone it takes to birth a book.

To my teachers and Spiritual Masters, Chief Joseph, St. Germain, Archangels Michael and Gabriel, Lady Nada, Lord Melchizedek, Lord Maitreya, and all the unnamed angels, guides and a star beings known and unknown to me who led me to this point of ascension, who directed me to say *Yes* to my destiny—I am honored to be in your service.

Most humbly and lovingly I thank you, Lord Sananda, for walking hand-in-hand with me on this earthly plane and endowing me with the privilege of being your chela and the divine vessel for Thy Will to flow through.

I love you All!

# $\mathcal{A}$BOUT THE $\mathcal{A}$UTHOR

Shima Shanti lived a healthy and wholesome life growing up in a large and lively family in Montana. Married to Jim Kelly for thirty-five years, together they lovingly raised their son, Jimmy, all the while following a many-faceted career path as corporate executive and entrepreneur.

In 2007, on this long path of self-discovery she came to know her God Presence and discovered her infinite Self *prior* to her birth in Coronado, California. Gracefully opening to enlightenment, Shima deepened her understanding of the ascension process through intense study and insight from the Spiritual realms. Realizing she was no longer bound by old karmic patterns, she found her Spiritual freedom to serve God and all His creation. Shima embarked on her path as teacher, servant and way shower.

Shima plays in all worlds simultaneously. She brings to Earth the many flavors of high frequencies in a mix never before tasted. Her diverse projects—writing spiritual guidebooks, opening stargates as a soul journeyer and sharing the *Ascension Keys*, SETTLEing STONES and other Peace Waters products through her enterprise www.PeaceWaters.com all serve to assist others on their ascension path.

Shima with her husband, Jim, balance their lives between San Diego, California and Whitefish, Montana savoring the simplicity of walking on the beach, hiking in the mountains and waiting for the next tap on the shoulder to serve.

# PEACE WATERS

**Peace Waters** products—Ascension Keys, SETTLEing STONES, Synergy Stones and Elohim Peace Waters—are the natural healing gifts of Mother Gaia. They are inspired, designed and co-created with the Elohim and Archangelic Messengers.

**The Peace Waters** tools assist individuals in their quest for heightened awareness and the shift in consciousness that open to exciting new energies and Divine realizations. Every product supports one's life energies and accelerates individual spiritual growth. The results are increased vitality, enhanced creativity and Peace.

For information on **Peace Waters** products and services, please visit our website: **www.peacewaters.com**.

www.ingramcontent.com/pod-product-compliance
Lightning Source LLC
Chambersburg PA
CBHW032304070726
47590CB00015B/485